The Christian Revolutionary

The
Christian Revolutionary

DALE W. BROWN

William B. Eerdmans Publishing Company
Grand Rapids, Michigan

TO
THE ECUMENICAL MOVEMENT FOR MANY RADICAL CHRISTIANS
—THE MANY COMMUNITIES FOR PEACE, FREEDOM,
AND JUSTICE IN OUR TIMES

Preface

*We are trying to live in an age of accelerating change with a
static theology. Since the phrase* rapid social change *serves
often merely as a euphemism for* revolution, *the issue could
be put even more bluntly: we are trying to live in a period
of revolution without a theology of revolution. The development of such a theology should be the first item of
the theological agenda today.* Harvey Cox, *The Secular City*

Throughout the debate about the death of God, I came to feel
strongly the need for a theology that more truly expresses the
radical nature of Christianity. This study is an attempt to fulfill
that need. It is an effort to provide a sound perspective for all
those who have been calling for a theology applicable to our
revolutionary times. Through my students, to whom I am deeply
indebted, I have become exposed to and involved in the idealism
and activity of the New Left. What follows represents in large
part a theological reflection on my involvement in that Movement.

Rather than adopt a systematic approach, I have chosen to
delineate radical and revolutionary themes by comparing my
definitions with those of other viewpoints that have co-opted the
label "radical." In doing so, I have discovered that I am very
much in dialogue both with my own distinct theological heritage
and with the broader theological context of the present century.
Even when it was less in vogue I tended to identify with the
radical rootage of my own sectarian background in the Church of
the Brethren. The chapter on the Social Gospel exhibits a basis in
American theology, for it was through Social Gospel liberalism

that Christianity first came alive for me as a youth. And though I did not identify fully with the death-of-God movement, I have as a contemporary theologian been struggling existentially in the same post-Barthian period of bewilderment and transition.

This book has evolved from the counsel of many. Besides my students I want especially to thank my colleagues Graydon Snyder and Robert Neff, biblical theologians at our seminary, for the meaningful ways in which the apocalyptic motifs of the Bible are coming alive for me. I wish to thank, too, the administration at Bethany Theological Seminary for lightening my responsibilities enough to allow me to complete this writing after a brief sabbatical leave. Finally, I shall always remain grateful to William Robert Miller, who initially encouraged me to write this book and who gave generously of his guidance in the organization of the chapters.

D.W.B.

Contents

CHAPTER I

What Is Radical Theology?

Radical and revolutionary theologizing, though anticipating something entirely new, has not emerged in a vacuum. Karl Barth's conjoining of Christology and creation was appropriated by the post-Barthian mind to affirm that in Christ God became secular or worldly. With Harvey Cox we came to celebrate the realization of biblical motifs in the technology, anonymity, and mobility of the secular city. We also found it exciting to analyze the possible meanings and implications of Bonhoeffer's fragments about "the world come of age." Since this mature world was one that could get along without the "god of the gaps" (the god we call upon to explain what we cannot otherwise fathom), the *deus ex machina* (the god who solves our problems and meets our needs), and the "religious god" (the god we domesticate for one sector of life), the death-of-God theologians celebrated the ultimate in secularization by pronouncing the death of the traditional God of metaphysics and Christendom.

The secular theologians affirm the world as the object of God's love and the locus of God's activity. But because of the obvious fallenness of the world, they are becoming increasingly aware that the world cannot be accepted as it is. One can celebrate certain aspects of the shape and style of the modern secular city, but at the same time, he must acknowledge its blight and alienation. One can celebrate the possibilities of cybernetics, but he must also deplore the fact that automation is currently more the handmaiden of exploitation, totalitarianism, and death than a tool for man's liberation. Idealists sallied forth from suburban churches to participate in God's activity in the world only to discover that responsible discipleship may mean opposing as well as working through the power structures of our society.

This great discrepancy between what might be and what is could have led to complete existential despair. Instead, we are experiencing a great revival of hope. Moving beyond the death-of-God theology and its rejection of the "God up there," the theologians of hope maintain a belief in the transcendent but point to a God who meets us in the historical possibilities we face. Far from soothing us with a futuristic eschatology of what will be in a utopian by-and-by, they preach a messianism that has the kingdom breaking into history now, in our own time, as an explosive force. It is this radical biblical expectation of the death of the old and the birth of the new which is speaking afresh in a revolutionary context. The context of Christian thought and life may be described as the world *coming* of age, rather than the world *come* of age. The world coming of age implies adolescent characteristics—awkward changes, an identity crisis challenging the old and appropriating the new, and stormy upheavals in the struggle of rival allegiances. The slogan of the secular theologians to let the world write the agenda has been heeded, and increasingly this agenda is being written by the revolutionary struggles of people to be free from exploitation, militarism, and elemental human wants.

It may be helpful to summarize this movement in theologizing: As secular theology affirmed, the object of God's love is the world, and therefore we too must love the world. But if we genuinely love the world, we cannot love it as it is. We must go beyond secularism. We as true believers will love the world so much that we want it to become what God intends it to be, the new kingdom and new humanity promised in Jesus Christ. This is the theology of hope. Living out this hopeful love means beginning now to participate in the kingdom God wills for all mankind—and here we arrive at the radical and revolutionary position.

RADICAL AS REVELATIONAL

Since the word "radical" was co-opted by the death-of-God theologians and readily applied to them by others, it is important to distinguish the senses of the term I have in mind. On the one hand I mean by "radical" that which is related to the root, that which is original, fundamental, and inherent. In this sense, instead of negating his faith, the Christian radical wants to get at the heart of it. Instead of attacking the church because its doctrine is passé, the new radicalism is more likely to oppose the church because it fails to put its beliefs into practice. "If Christians are to know again for what reasons they are here," says Jürgen Moltmann, "they must also rediscover who they really are."[1]

For Karl Barth being a Christian is still determined by the life of Jesus, regarded as the revelation of the ultimate. And for Dietrich Bonhoeffer that revelation occurs concretely in "Christ existing as community." God discloses himself within the historic community stemming from the Christ-event. The Spirit of Jesus comes to us through the lives of other people. The hermeneutical function of neoorthodoxy, which stressed the historical rootedness of the Christian faith, may still be to enliven and make sense out of traditional biblical themes. Those who are doing theology today from a historicist perspective, see in the life and death of the man on the cross the supreme paradigm of the nature of reality.[2]

Theologians of hope rightly criticize any perspective that would define Christianity as a backward-looking movement. They are suspicious of passionate efforts to regain "paradise lost." But while it is true that attempts to reproduce the life style of Jesus or the "golden age" of the early church may be deceptive and futile, the *imitatio Christi* theme and the pre-Constantinian church have in fact provided a powerful dynamic for Christian life through the centuries. Moltmann, who has opposed such preoccupation with pristine origins, also acknowledges the great place the analogies of the past have had in revitalizing hope in the future.[3] For the faith in man's moving through history to new possibilities has its basis in the linear philosophy of history espoused by the prophets of old.

Because of their interest in roots, theological radicals have affinities with religious conservatives. Just as the political left and right are often together in their desire to restore decentralization, personal freedom, and constitutional rights, so the theological left and right share similar biblical concerns about the universal priesthood, the revolutionary power of the gospel, anti-institutionalism, and Christian hope. But there are fundamental differences in the way radicals and conservatives regard the beginnings. In examining and questioning his beliefs, the radical of the left does not fear as much as his brother on the right that removing one stone will destroy the Christian faith. He does agree with Bishop Robinson, however, that the radical must be a man of tradition, for without roots "he is unlikely to have the security to question to the depths."[4]

RADICAL AS REVOLUTIONARY

This brings us to a second definition of "radical." The word not only relates to roots but can also mean a departure from the usual, a considerable deviation from the traditional. Radical actions are thoroughgoing, extreme, drastic. Radicalism implies a fundamental departure from or challenge to the status quo. It is revolutionary. These two definitions may seem contradictory. How can a return to the roots of a tradition be consistent with a fundamental departure from that tradition? The answer, of course, is that a tradition can deviate from its roots. Thus returning to the source of the faith may entail challenging the church and society of the present. A recovery of revelation may be revolutionary.

The words "revolutionary" and "revolution" are even more confusing and of more diverse use than "radical." The root *revolvere* means "roll back or again." Its astronomical origins referred to the perpetual return of a celestial body, the completion of a cycle. Revolution as rolling back to the starting point parallels the radical course of returning to the roots. But the moment the cycle is completed, it begins again. The rotation and change are continual. Even more than "radical," "revolutionary" has come through the years to mean sudden change. Politically, the word even connotes violence. But revolution does not necessarily require violence, as we see when Madison Avenue dubs a new product "revolutionary."

A great many biblical and theological themes are revolutionary. The prophetic motif of promise and fulfillment has affinities with the original meaning of revolution in that what is often anticipated is a return to the promised land. The motif of death and resurrection, however, connotes the coming of something completely new. Revolutionary change is implied in the doctrines of the new birth, the new creation, and a new heaven and earth. Many of these common biblical themes will be expanded later. The most complicated theological definition of revolution I have encountered is one by a Princeton graduate student: "Revolution consists in the actualization of the promise of revelation proleptically appropriated by means of the paradigm acting as a function of the future."[5] More simply this may mean that when the biblical promises come alive for us to the extent that we really believe and act as if they will be fulfilled, then there will be a revolution.

It is commonly noted today that we live in a post-Constantinian age. But rather than bemoan the church's loss of influence and the demise of cultural Christianity, the radical mind welcomes the change. In fact, because disenchanted youth are making sense to some in their assertion that the powers-that-be have not been spectacularly successful in their management of the world, a case is being made for a theology and a community that is counter-establishment, and in that sense counter-cultural. Such a theology is offered by John Pairman Brown in his book *The Liberated Zone: A Guide to Christian Resistance.* Radical and revolutionary theologies represent efforts to formulate a position against "this monolithic political-industrial-military-propagandist complex."[6]

THE DIALECTIC OF THE OLD AND THE NEW

Our dual definition of radical theology as both revelational and revolutionary may offer something to both sides of the growing chasm of our time. Peter Berger in a *Christian Century* article depicts this polarization as between those who fear chaos and those who fear tyranny.[7] Those who fear chaos want earnestly to preserve the old values and the old ways. They experience great anxiety in reading of riots, of a growing crime rate, and of militant youth. Disturbed by the new morality and by changes on every hand, they feel that everything which has been nailed down is coming loose. Normal life and orderly government threaten to disintegrate. It is no longer safe to walk through a city park by night. Responding to this fear, many major politicians have conducted mayoralty and congressional campaigns as if they were running for sheriff. Now consistent with our definition, true radicals will never rejoice in the collapse of what has been best in our civilization; they will empathize with those who fear chaos and work to maintain those values which have been most Christian and humane.

At the same time, our definition of radicalism supports those who fear tyranny. These people are justifiably impatient with our gross injustices at home and our tacit approval of colonialism around the world. They demand a new order. Failure to grant freedom now is tyranny. Failure to achieve a more equitable division of the world's great material abundance is immorality and violence of the worst kind. Those who fear tyranny are outraged by the apparent loss of liberties by those who protest against militarism and by those who effectively work for self-determination in ghetto communities. They are alarmed by the growing chauvinism and spirit of fascism in American life. Christian radicals will participate in this revolutionary challenge to the status quo.

To affirm what is best in both of these views, a dialectic between the old and the new, is basic to the biblical perspective. The Old Testament prophets called Israel to return to its basic covenant at the same time they attacked the status quo in the name of the same covenant. "Return, O Israel, to the Lord your God" (Hos. 14:1-2) is matched by another prophetic call: "Behold, I am doing a new thing; now it springs forth, do you not perceive it?" (Isa. 43:19). In the New Testament the Pauline admonition to "hold fast what is good" (1 Thess. 5:21) is held with the promise: "Behold I make all things new" (Rev. 21:5). The early Christians were more intent on fulfilling the law than destroying it; yet, they were described as those who were turning the world upside down.

At its best the church through history has fulfilled both roles. It has preserved basic values from the past, and at the same time its message and life have served as a catalyst to spawn revolutionary challenges to the status quo. When anarchy has threatened, there have been movements in the church to provide meaning and order to men's lives. On the other hand, when society has been set in its ways, Christian voices have arisen to challenge the accepted presuppositions of the culture. When the church has departed from its message, voices have boldly called her back to her roots. When the church has been at ease in Zion, the Christian faith has displayed an unusual capacity for disruption. A crisis in the collective life of man may send a man seeking the revolutionary stuff of the Bible. An intimate familiarity with the biblical proclamation may energize him for the revolutionary task of changing the present state of affairs. Today, we live in a period in which those who preach the preservation of that which is good need to dialogue with those who are passionately anticipating the coming of the new. As the differences are faced, an awareness might emerge of the possibilities of mutual relatedness. For the church must fight rear-guard action against the destruction of its roots at the same time it continues to send forth avant-garde troops engaged in innovative and revolutionary enterprises.

Because of this revelational-revolutionary dialectic, radical theology is not satisfied with either a conservative or a liberal tag. Theologically, as well as politically, the lines of the conservative-liberal debate are not as neatly drawn and meaningful as they were in the recent past. The radical can identify with the conservative's desire to preserve the faith. But he cannot agree with some who so emphasize the *personal* Savior as to mitigate his being Lord over *all* of life. Neither can the radical agree with those who equate Christianity with American foreign policy or the American way of life. On the other hand, as youthful political radicals lay the sad state of our country at the feet of the liberal establishment more than at the feet of the conservatives, so young theological radicals have come to sense that more than the conservative is the enemy. Though admired for his social teachings and his doctrine of openness, the liberal is accused of teaching peace and brotherhood while being an integral part of those structures which make for war. He is charged with hypocrisy, compromise, and anemic witness. In the struggles of our period between the privileged and the dispossessed, the liberal's objective stance as a reconciler of differences has sometimes been more a traditional ecclesiastical triumphalism than a participation with God in his sufferings in the world.

Because it is a different ball game than the fundamentalist-liberal rivalry, we may be in for some surprises in the new lineups. Inter-Varsity political leftists may seem to be an anomaly to many, but not to growing numbers of evangelical radicals. To increasing numbers of youth in South America, Pentecostalism and revolutionary goals are not antithetical. The Young Friends of North America represent a strange, yet perhaps natural union of evangelical Quakerism with radical social protest. It was surprising to discover that many theological students in West Berlin are Maoists. Should the claim to be a Christian Maoist, however, be regarded as more contradictory than the assertion that one is a Christian capitalist? All such labels, including the many theological varieties, have their limitations and dangers. Nevertheless, we use them to differentiate our varying interpretations of the faith and to avoid presumptuously naming as Christian our own particular configurations. Here I wish only to argue that "radical" describes more accurately the mood of many than do some other labels.

THEOLOGY FOR REVOLUTION

I do not mean to suggest that an esoteric cadre of theologians and students has been devising radical and revolutionary theologies as a way to spawn a revolution. On the contrary, we have found ourselves in the midst of revolution and have been wondering how to react to it. It is trite to say but momentous to fully grasp the fact that we live in a revolutionary situation. In a world which has the capacity for material abundance, we have a system in which the rich grow richer and the poor, poorer. In a world of potential technological mastery, we have false priorities. The amount of money spent on armaments by a few major powers is equal to the total national income of the combined continents of Central and South America, Africa, and Asia.

Revolutionary ferment has exuded from black power groups, disenfranchised students, third-world guerrilla forces, and the masses of the dispossessed themselves. Many churchmen, liberals, idealists, and intellectuals have been radicalized as their efforts to achieve social justice through normal channels have been rebuffed. Vietnam and the urban ghettoes have demonstrated that the fundamental ills of our society are not minor maladjustments to be remedied through a mild and quiet tinkering with the system. Rather, the controlling institutional structures of society themselves represent a threat to the well-being of all mankind. On those days when my liberal background predominates, I like to feel that our present plight is one which will soon pass away as our system rectifies and effects the necessary adjustments. On other days, it seems that our society is on the verge of blowing up as a cataclysmic prelude to the coming of something new.

The revolutionary consciousness which has emerged, then, is a radical apprehension of how minimally Christian the present social order is and how desperately it needs to be changed. It is true, of course, that gross injustices and inequalities have always existed. And attempts to explain the restlessness of university youth are typically countered with the remark: "Someday they will wake up and realize that the world has always been this way and always will be." The generation gap may well be the result of a heightened belief in the revolutionary claim that the world must be changed and things cannot continue as they always have. Following a graphic critique of our situation, James Douglass concludes: "In such a world, revolution is not a question and a possibility. It is an obligation and a necessity." He proposes that in our kind of world the revolutionary may be the contemporary man of conscience.[8]

Because we already live in the midst of a social revolution, some voices stress the need of a theology *for* revolution rather than a theology *of* revolution. Paul Lehmann defines such a theology as "an analytical undertaking that tries, by conceptual means, to explore the bearing of the relation between messianism and humanization upon the fact and the dynamics of revolutionary social change."[9] Lehmann believes that the framework for such a theology today is the occasion presented by Marxism and Leninism. Rather than committing itself to revolutionary schemes and ideologies of its own, theologizing should, he feels, be a dynamic conceptual *response* to the occasion presented by history in an effort to make it more human.

Such a definition mitigates against any attempt to set up a "Christian revolution." Just as there can be no "Christian" political parties—those adopting this designation have floundered in explaining the relationship of their name to their nature—so there cannot be a "Christian revolution." In a major address at the 1966 World Council of Churches Conference on Church and Society at Geneva, Professor Heinz-Dietrich Wendland emphasized that Christians "do not set up any 'Christian' orders, systems, states and societies; for their task is to *humanise* the secular orders, and the slightest real progress that can be attained there is more important than the most perfect Christian Utopia, because it guarantees real help to definite people or social groups."[10] For the Christian, human revolutionary schemes and ideologies will not be absolutized but will always be subject to the judgment of the coming of the kingdom.

Though there can be no "Christian revolution," a Christian can become a revolutionary. The Christian should not put on every faddish revolutionary style that comes along. At the same time he should not be merely a spectator watching from the street. Because he believes in the reality of the coming kingdom of God, he is free to participate in, indeed abandon himself to, the signs of its arrival. And because he refuses to absolutize any human ideologies, he is ready to appropriate the judgment of God on himself as well as on the oppressors. In some respects, the Christian may be called to be *in* the revolution but not *of* it.

THEOLOGY OF REVOLUTION

The advent of theologies for revolution means that Christians do respond to historical situations. Through the eyes of faith, however, they also believe that the power of the gospel may bring something new. The radical perspective in theology has emerged not merely as a response to the empirical world, but also from an attempt to follow the revolutionary motifs of the biblical witness. A revolutionary hermeneutic is emerging, one which views the biblical material, for the most part, to have been written in a revolutionary situation on behalf of the dispossessed by a community with worldly apocalyptic expectations. Be it faddism or be it a correct reading of the dynamic biblical perspective, the participants in the Conference on Church and Society represent a growing desire to develop a theology of revolution.

Whether one accepts the presuppositions of a revolutionary hermeneutic or not, it will be necessary to be in conversation with the exegetical conclusions. For current reflections on many biblical themes focus on the revolutionary nature of the gospel. It is maintained that in the biblical tradition the name for God is revolutionary. *Yahweh* is derived from a root suggesting "to become or to come to pass." The doctrine of creation out of nothing points to a dynamic revolutionary perspective which is change-oriented rather than preservation-oriented. The prophetic theme of promise and fulfillment does not depict the movement of history so much in terms of a neat evolutionary course as in terms of judgment and tearing down, salvation and building up. The central Exodus motif is one of a deliverance from political enslavement and the sending forth of a pilgrim people into a new history.

With the coming of Christianity we have the proclamation of the New Testament or covenant, the new Israel, the new man, the new wine, a new song, the new Jerusalem, a new heaven and earth, and the promise: "Behold I make all things new" (Rev. 21:5). The doctrine of repentance indicates that the Christian life begins in crisis. The biblical concepts of rebirth, new life, and conversion point to a fundamental change—from sin to grace, from selfishness to love. The doctrine of conversion applied to all of life may well lead to a theology of revolution. The cross discloses that reconciliation is impossible apart from suffering. Death and resurrection, the death of the old and the birth of the new, is a basic revolutionary motif, perhaps more existentially understood by many pagan participants in the struggles of our time than by respectable members in the fold. Apocalypticism, messianism, and eschatology are being revived and reinterpreted by biblical scholars in such a way as to bring the future into the present as a dynamic, living, political reality. In the theological halls of ivy there is a new marriage between eschatology and ethics. Christian social ethics now depicts the Christian life style as more radical and revolutionary than did the neoorthodox era of greater ambiguities and so-called biblical realism.

So concerned is Jürgen Moltmann to focus attention on the eschatological that he is unsatisfied with such words as "reformation," "renewal," "revival," and "revolution." He maintains that the "re" prefix makes them basically reactionary. They turn us backward, they speak of a return to a previous point, they place our goal behind us. Though not many will be guilty of this literalism, Moltmann tries to insure that the human dream is turned forward by proposing that we substitute "provolution" for "revolution."[11] Resurrection, in this perspective, points to new possibilities rather than a recapitulation of the old.

More prevalent than this worry is a concern that since revolution either anticipates or represents the *completion* of a successful rebellion, the term may be too static. It may represent an absolutizing of the new situation gained by the rebellion and simply identify Christianity with a new status quo. Rolland Smith prefers the concept of rebellion itself, which he defines as "a continual revolution. . .ever in process of being established."[12] Yet, because this term has negative connotations, Smith's concern might better be met by speaking of the need for a doctrine of "permanent revolution."

Somewhat akin to the pitfall of absolutizing a revolution is the peril of apostasy. Instead of identifying Christianity with the revolution, the Christian may become so enthusiastically involved in the struggle and so disillusioned with establishment Christianity that he comes to forsake the faith. The call to participate in God's activity in history always presents the problem of discerning where and how God is working. Since God may not be on the side of every revolutionary, the Christian needs the transcending vision of the kingdom to judge the revolution and his participation in it.

REVOLUTION IN THEOLOGY

It is true to the spirit of our times that there has emerged the slogan that there should be no theology of revolution until there is a revolution in theology. As young radicals are becoming skeptical of intellectual theorists who do not lay their bodies on the line, so many will not be impressed with theological formulations unless there is some evidence that those who theologize are in some way involved in the revolution. Increasingly, theology will be judged more by its fruits than by the soundness of its position, however important the latter may remain. The church has no business expounding a theology of revolution unless it is in the business of revolutionizing its own life and mission. As a theology of personal conversion was appropriate for the American frontier, so a theology of social conversion may be the way the Word comes alive in an era of revolutionary ferment. Where we may respond to the changing times by formulating theologies for and of revolution, it is best to heed the admonition given at a recent gathering of young seminarians. It was affirmed there that the Christian should not claim the title of revolutionary for himself. Rather by God's grace he should live in such a way that such a designation will be applied to him by friends and foes alike.

CHAPTER II

The Radical Reformation – Then and Now

Given the current emphasis on radical and revolutionary themes, it is not surprising that there is renewed interest in the sectaries and radicals of the past. I have listened to veterans of ecumenism deplore the sectarianism prevalent among the youth of the World Council of Churches. Theologians of the Roman Catholic Left, such as Michael Novak and Rosemary Ruether, not only champion radical ecclesiological motifs and revolutionary change but identify the historical antecedents of their message with the Radical Reformation of the sixteenth century.[1] Richard Shaull, one of the leading American apologists for a revolutionary theology, is calling for a rediscovery in church and in society of the meaning of our sectarian heritage.[2]

As an aid in further defining the radical mood, therefore, it may be helpful to compare contemporary expressions of radical witness with expressions of the past. It would be profitable, no doubt, to examine the Franciscan protest within the medieval church or the Waldensian schism from the church, the militant and pacifist wings of the Hussite revolution in Bohemia, or the fascinating sectarian groups coming from Russian Christianity in the nineteenth century. However, the focus here will be on the radical or left wing of the sixteenth-century Reformation, with a lesser emphasis on the subsequent radical movements coming into prominence a century later in Puritan England. Such a dialogue should sharpen the issues involved in formulating a Christian posture toward society and in delineating the proper shape of the church in a revolutionary era.

THE POST-CONSTANTINIAN SITUATION

There is a growing consensus that Christendom today may be facing a crisis in some ways similar to the situation at the time of the Reformation. The institutional crisis of Christendom in the sixteenth century is seen most vividly in the phenomenon known as the Left-Wing or Radical Reformation. Including such diverse groups as the Anabaptists, the Spiritualists, the Anti-Trinitarians, and the militant Revolutionaries, the Radical Reformers all repudiated the millennium of cultural synthesis known as the *Corpus Christianum*, in which the church and human society coincided numerically. The empire was regarded as holy; the church was the empire at prayer. The *Corpus Christianum* had emerged when, after three centuries of persecution, the Emperor Constantine began to favor Christianity. Rising from an illegal sect to a tolerated religion in the Edict of Milan, A.D. 313, Christianity became the only tolerated religion by 392, when the Emperor Theodosius forbade all pagan worship, public and private, under penalty of death. In opposition to the traditional view espoused by Eusebius, which has seen Constantine's conversion as the glorious beginning of the Christianization of the world, the Radical Reformers located the fall of the church in its alignment with the interests of the empire.

Owing to the rise of Anabaptist historiography in the last few decades, we are now able to ascertain the posture of the Radical Reformers not merely through the polemical utterances of their opponents but through their own words. The challenge to the *Corpus Christianum* was not limited to the armed revolutionary action of Thomas Müntzer during the Peasants' War of 1525 or the armed Anabaptist theocracy at Münster a decade later. From the beginning of the movement in 1525, religious toleration and the separation of church and state were advocated by Anabaptists who were pacifist. Although the militant radicals may appear to have been the more revolutionary in their aims and actions, they in a sense represented a continuation of the Constantinian union of church and state since they tried to enforce by the sword their own configuration of Christianity. More truly revolutionary were those Anabaptists who believed that both church and state should repudiate force in religious matters and that joining the *Corpus Christi* was a matter of choice.

Yet, though nonviolent and obedient to the state in temporal matters, these pacifist Anabaptists were considered by the Establishment of their day to be as subversive as the violent revolutionaries. On the other hand, in their desire to have us carefully differentiate between the peaceful Swiss Anabaptists and the Münsterites, Anabaptist scholars have often gone too far in denying the inner relationship between Anabaptism and the revolutionary ferment of the time. Walter Klassen's corrective is to the point:

> There can be no doubt that the Anabaptists, with the exception of the Münster episode and a few other minor incidents, were nonviolent. They did not think of or plan violent revolution. Nevertheless, by the canons of the time, the assumptions, understanding, and actions of the peaceful Anabaptists could only be interpreted as revolution, although only the first stages. . . .After all, Anabaptists refused to acknowledge ultimate authority in popes, magistrates and reformers in a day that took absolutisms for granted. . . .Their assumptions and actions were in fact destructive of the whole religio-social structure of the time. . . .The charge of incipient revolution was therefore in a measure justified.[3]

The truth is that the Establishment of the sixteenth century, including the main-line Reformers, their princes, and the Roman Catholics, could not conceive of society's holding together apart from the cement of a unifying faith. The possibility of religious pluralism posed the threat of anarchy. The Anabaptists were regarded in the same light as many Americans view radicals today.

The word "Anabaptism," which literally means "re-baptism," was applied to the movement by the Establishment. The Swiss

Brethren themselves rejected this concept since they refused to acknowledge their first baptism, as infants in the state churches, as any baptism at all. In their rejection of the *Corpus Christianum*, they saw baptism without the consent of the infant recipient as a violation of religious freedom as well as a denial of the confessional nature of dying and rising in Christ. But the charge "anabaptist" was zealously applied by the authorities because they wanted to revive the death penalty decreed in the Justinian Code of 529 for two heresies—anti-trinitarianism and re-baptism. Severe and systematic persecution was pursued. Anabaptists were mutilated, tortured, burned, drowned, or exiled. Believers' baptism in the sixteenth century, then, represented more than a difference in biblical interpretation; it indicated a radical rejection of the *Corpus Christianum* and an entirely new view of the church. Being baptized into one of the new brotherhoods was in reality more dangerous, subversive, and revolutionary than burning a draft card in twentieth-century America.

The rejection of the *Corpus Christianum* by the Radical Reformers carried many implications for the nature of the *Corpus Christi*. If one no longer accepts the equation of Christianity with society, then one begins to think in terms of two entities, church and world, the pilgrim people and Babel. If the church is to be separate from the state, then the magistrate can no longer dictate what the conscience must accept. If one does not automatically become a member of the community of faith at birth, a missionary psychology is inevitable. In fact, one's own children must be wooed through persuasion and preaching. This repudiation of the *Corpus Christianum* and the corresponding affirmation of the *Corpus Christi* channelled into the stream of Christian history disciplined new brotherhoods formed by the gathering of confessing believers.

Today, there is an increasing consciousness that we may again be living in a post-Constantinian situation. Our era is being named "post-Christian." Some feel that Thomas J. J. Altizer's atheism, which is deeply religious and not devoid of God-talk, describes more accurately the death of the God of Christendom than the death of the God of the Bible.[4] But how can our situation be described as post-Constantinian in a land which has never been Constantinianized? The American Constitution separated church and state, and we have never experienced the *Corpus Christianum* as rigidly as a country in which a state church predominates. Nevertheless, we have known factory churches, Bible-reading in public schools, and prayer breakfasts for Congressmen. Though many of the founding fathers were deists and most of the first settlers were venturesome pagans, the myth of a "Christian" America has served as a powerful dynamic in our national life. The fruits of the American *Corpus Christianum* have been the attempts to legislate Puritan versions of Christian morality and the Constantinian heresy that reverts to a pagan view of God as a national deity.

There are many signs of the worldwide demise of that notion of *Corpus Christianum* erected on the success of eighteenth- and nineteenth-century revivals and missions. Missionary strategists are repudiating the traditional view which classifies some nations as Christian and others as pagan. It is affirmed that every Christian lives in a missionary situation. Churchmen in Communist countries extol the virtues of disestablishment. Increasing numbers of pastors in the main-line churches of Europe question their establishment role as statisticians of births, marriages, and deaths. The increasing debate over the validity of infant baptism is but a symptom of a widespread disenchantment with the status quo. In America, it is predicted that if present trends continue, by the turn of the century only 12 per cent of the population will be supporting the prosperous church institutions of the present. The churches are having to face the great plurality of rival world views and are forced to deal with the polarizations that are coming to characterize American life. Some are pronouncing the fall of the church because it simply reflects the culture; others are threatening to bolt from the church because prophetic voices are beginning to challenge the culture.

The current deconstantinizing of the church may lead in interesting directions. If Christianity once again loses its respectability, a revolutionary prophetic community may emerge. If to be a Christian is no longer a status symbol, commitment may become more genuine and radical. If institutional Christianity diminishes in power and influence, the life together may grow more bold in witness and posture. If the church is no longer regarded as the bulwark of society, it may again feel more affinities with the minorities which constituted the New Testament church.

THE PRE-CONSTANTINIAN MYTH

As the post-Constantinian situation is congenial to our formulation of radicalism as confronting the status quo, the accompanying myth about the pre-Constantinian church fits our other definition of radical as returning to the roots. If the fall of the church occurred with Constantine's patronage and baptism, then it is assumed that the kind of church which existed before the fall was desirable. All traditions to some extent affirm the early Christian community as normative. The Catholic and Orthodox world reserves a special place for the early fathers, and proponents of biblical authority often derive the special place they give to the canonical documents from the fact that the writers were close to the key events and their proclamation by the community of faith. Historically, Christian radicals of many varieties have been attracted to the idea of returning to the faith and life of the early Christians. Francis of Assisi and his followers set out to mimic the poverty, dress, and life style of Jesus and the early disciples. The Unity of Czech Brethren consciously wished to return to the spirit of the apostolic church. William Penn was fond of viewing Quakerism as "Primitive Christianity Revived." Gottfried Arnold's *Portrayal of the First Christians* (1696) had a wide influence in radical Protestant circles. Most scholars place this desire to restore the faith and life of the early church as a basic ingredient in Anabaptist theology. This motif has been variously referred to as restitutionism, primitivism, restorationism, and apostolicity.

I have referred to the *myth* of the pre-Constantinian church in order to point out that this view is not entirely accurate and that we are dealing in large part with an issue of faith which cannot be demonstrated, or disproved, by historical research. Among the most common attacks on the restitutionist view has been a rejection of the notion that the early church was above reproach. One has only to be aware of the issues involved in Paul's correspondence with the Corinthian church to recognize that the early church was not constituted by morally pure, doctrinally sound, well-ordered members. Even though it is countered that it is the shape and style of life in the early church that is to be imitated, rather than any moral purity, there are still many problems in discerning whether first-century polity has much relevance for Christians in a technological age.

I have already cited the more basic objection to such a backward look made by Moltmann and others. For these theologians of hope such efforts to return to the security of pristine origins contradict the fundamental nature of the Christian faith. Faith in the resurrection, it is maintained, means a forward look, an expectation of the coming of the new. Nevertheless, for Moltmann the myths and analogies of the past do have a great place in revitalizing hope in the reality of the future. It is my contention that this has been precisely the case with the radical movements. Young Mennonite scholars who sought to recover the Anabaptist vision were not simply seeking to reproduce the past. In seeking to define who they had been, they were criticizing who they were and formulating a vision of who they should become. The same dynamic has characterized most primitivists. In examining Christian origins, radicals have consciously and unconsciously been pointing to the new shape of the church of the future. Moltmann himself has recognized that the wish to regain primordial origins has often given birth to a new epoch in history.[5] In a real sense all theologians of hope who return to the biblical materials for examples of eschatological witness are primitivists of a kind. The Anabaptist scholar John Howard Yoder has asserted that when the word "restitution" was used by the Reformation Radicals, "this meant not a simple repetition of what had been before, but rather a positive movement forward in the history of salvation through the overcoming of apostasy, which brought the church farther along than it had been in the simplicity of the first century."[6]

It may be helpful to acknowledge that other ways of stressing the rootedness of the faith also lack exact historical verification. The idea of apostolic succession, for example, cannot be historically validated. It is difficult to demonstrate that there has been an unbroken succession of authority from the beginning such as to substantiate a particular view of hierarchical authority. Such a picture of historical continuity, however, can serve as a powerful and meaningful myth. In struggling with the same problem of locating the true church, spiritualists such as Sebastian Franck and the main-line Reformers could not find it either in the early church or in contemporary forms. They concluded that the true church remained invisible. The Anabaptists refused to identify the visible church with a hierarchical division of a monolithic society. But they were not satisfied with the idea of an invisible mystic communion of true believers. Rather, they opted for a visible disciplined community to be differentiated from society. And in so doing, they drew inspiration from their myth about the style of faith and life of the early church.

This preoccupation with the relation of the early community to their own brotherhoods was reflected in Anabaptist hermeneutics. With the main-line Reformers they shifted the locus of authority from sacerdotal interpreters to the inspired text. But unlike these right-wing Reformers, who depended upon technically qualified theological experts, the Anabaptists relied on the community of faith. Their pattern was the rule of Paul as expressed in I Corinthians 14:29: "Let two or three prophets speak, and let the others weigh what is said." Their hermeneutical principle was simply that the text is best understood in a congregation.[7] This was novel in the sixteenth century even though the Anabaptists claimed it to be but a logical application of the doctrine of the priesthood or "theologianhood" of all believers.

The emphasis of the radicals on the *Corpus Christi* may have some points of contact with the findings of the form critics. Asserting that the biblical materials have come to us more in the form of the proclamation and faith of the early community than as matter of fact history, form criticism has played havoc with some theories of verbal inspiration. But this emphasis on community sayings and social occurrences has heightened the necessity to understand the community of faith as the context for the biblical message.

Today, with the great interest in community life styles, corporate celebration, group dynamics, and underground churches, there may emerge a growing interest in the New Testament church. And as we find apostolicity in the faith and style of the early community, so we will sense that our historical continuity with the early church is through those known and unknown, visible, prophetic, sectarian, allegedly heretical, underground, and gathered communities of the faithful through the centuries.

COUNTERCOMMUNITIES

The rejection of the Constantinian synthesis, a synthesis the radicals felt to have paganized the church more than it christianized culture, along with the acceptance of the myth about the situation of the primitive church, resulted in a new posture vis-à-vis the state. Though accused as anarchists and plotters of revolution, the Anabaptists shared with the main-line Reformers a belief in the divine origin of the state. Because of the sinfulness of man, the state was regarded as necessary. It was God's answer to human sin. The chief function of the officers of government was to maintain order. Consistent with this Reformation view of the state, the Anabaptists appropriated the biblical texts defining the power of government to punish the wicked and protect the good. Their fundamental departure from the prevailing view came in formulating the limitation of the government's power. Whereas for the classical Reformers the state was the defender of faith, the punishment of dissenters being necessary for the preservation of order, the Anabaptists denied the authority of the state in the spiritual realm. Because faith cannot be compelled, they believed that government oversteps its function when it attempts to rule over conscience.[8]

Since, according to the radical view, the primary role of the state is to preserve the necessary social cohesion to make possible the spread of the good news, it is necessary to have counter-communities that are free from the coercive hand of the state in matters of faith. The religious liberty which the Anabaptists sought for themselves should, they insisted, also be granted to others—even to Jews and Turks, a truly revolutionary position in the sixteenth century.[9] In the common life of the counter-communities, it was taught that obedience to the legitimate functions of civil government in matters of law and order was a part of the obedience Christians owe to God. Even obedience to a bad government might be an expression of thanksgiving to God for providing a relatively ordered context. Since they strove to separate their communities from the state, however, their obedience related only to those functions of the state they judged to be legitimate. In the case of directives they considered beyond the jurisdiction of the state, they argued the primacy of God's commands. Claus Felbinger, an early Anabaptist, stated this view in his confession:

> Therefore we are gladly and willingly subject to the government for the Lord's sake, and in all just matters we will in no way oppose it. When, however, the government requires of us what is contrary to our faith and conscience—as swearing oaths and paying hangman's dues or taxes for war—then we do not obey its command.[10]

As the confession indicates, refusing to take an oath was considered noncooperation. The Anabaptists based their position on the necessity to follow Christ's command and on the fact that one cannot be certain of fulfilling his promises since only God controls the future. Undoubtedly underlying this reason was, among other things, a desire to be free of any legalistic rendition of the Old Testament covenant. A more radical mark of separation and noncooperation was the Anabaptist view that Christians could not resort to the sword, not in the defense of social order or even in the conduct of a just war. Thus, since the pacifist Anabaptists saw the use of the sword as inherent in the role of government, they held that no true Christian could hold civil office. Though the state was divinely instituted by God, its functions were not to be legitimatized for Christian involvement. In early Dutch Anabaptism and later developments, however, it was conceded that Christians could participate in those aspects of government primarily engaged in promoting the good.

This separatist stance of countercommunities vis-à-vis the Establishment has meaningful points of contact with our own situation. The legacy of religious liberty speaks to a generation fighting for the right of conscience to oppose the status quo. The principle of voluntarism as a way to join together is relevant in an era repudiating authoritarianisms and looking for new ways to come to community through consensus. The Anabaptist refusal to take the required oath before the magistrate offers a powerful paradigm to those who are attempting to challenge the pagan tribal cult which identifies Americanism with Christianity. In spite of its demise among Anabaptists, even the stance which disavows participating in politics and holding public office now makes more sense than it did for several generations. For many are feeling that a truer witness might be made by not voting than by receiving a red feather for voting in a contest in which no real options are available. Likewise, young radicals have taught us anew the validity and perhaps the ultimate relevance of activity outside the power structures in preference to the compromises which so often accompany participation inside.

In spite of this valuable legacy, however, some of us are troubled by the sharp church-world dualism which often comes through implicitly or explicitly in Anabaptist apologetics. The biblical scholars have taught us that the message of the gospel proclaims Christ as Lord of all the world and not merely the church. Experientially, we are aware of how much the fallen world becomes a part of the life of even the most exemplary and dedicated community. This dualism between a pure, pacifist church and an evil, violent world has led some Anabaptist communities to keep their hands clean while the world goes to hell. An old Anabaptist elder in a community in Canada, for example, was pure in his insistence that no Christian could fight. At the same time, he was glad the Americans were fighting to protect his group from the evil Communist forces.

Such a view can preserve a realism which recognizes that nations will not quickly adopt the way of suffering love, but it has too easily resulted in a quietism which has refused to challenge the society with the witness that the lordship of Christ extends over the powers and principalities. Too often, Anabaptists have remained silent when the rights of others were threatened. It is when the state encroaches on their religious freedom that they have been most ready to offer passive resistance. Likewise, Anabaptists have failed to prophetically challenge the state when it has violated its own commission of punishing the evil and protecting the good. For the state truly becomes demonic when it turns its own mandate upside down by punishing the innocent and rewarding the guilty. Such selectivity is seen in the testimony of Claus Felbinger, who would pay some taxes but refused to pay the hangman's dues or taxes for war. On this issue Anabaptists have been divided from the beginning. I should like to maintain that the separation of countercommunities from the control of the state should not lead to indifference and passivity on the part of the Christian but to active witness to the lordship of Christ over powers and principalities.

THE DISCIPLINED COMMUNITY

Countercommunities can quickly become sectarian in the dictionary sense of being narrowly confined to a particular group or dogma. But "sectarian" is also derived from a root meaning "to follow." In a Christian context, then, "sectarian" can mean "following Jesus," or "discipleship." It is this affirmation of

Christianity as discipleship that Harold S. Bender, one of the pivotal figures in Anabaptist historiography, saw as central to the Anabaptist vision. For him the attempt to recover primitive Christianity, the view of the church as brotherhood, and the ethic of love and nonresistance were but natural outgrowths of the theme of discipleship.[11] As the theological climate shifts today from ministering to man's anxiety to calling for responsible participation in the world, discipleship is reappearing as a major theme. And the other side of discipleship is discipline, both etymologically and practically.

From the instructions outlined in Matthew 18 for settling differences, the Anabaptists adopted the ban as the means of discipline. The lesser ban, exclusion from communion, and the greater ban, excommunication from membership, were effected by the consensus of the brotherhood rather than by the magistrate or priest. It must be remembered that the ban was formulated in the context of the practice of the state churches, who called upon the magistrate to punish by death or exile those who were guilty of doctrinal or ecclesiastical deviations. This liberalization and humanization of the methods of that day is indicated in the rationale offered by the Schleitheim Confession: "In the perfection of Christ, however, only the ban is used for a warning and for the excommunication of the one who has sinned, without putting to death—simply the warning and the command to sin no more."[12] In addition, the ban could have been an expedient measure to protect the hunted and persecuted brotherhoods from wanton infiltration. At its best, discipline was for the welfare and restoration of the wayward brother. It was part of a spirit of mutual concern and of sharing with any in need. The brotherhood felt that when it used the ban it was only confirming and dealing with an alienation that had already taken place. It is true, however, that when brotherhood disappears discipline in sectarian groups can easily become punitive rather than redemptive, mechanical rather than personal.

Today there is a new hunger for the style of discipline that accompanies genuine commitment or discipleship. Heeding the wave of criticisms of acculturated Christianity, many congregations are struggling with ways to make church membership more meaningful. A few church-renewal pastors are beginning to report the positive fruits of their ministry in terms of how many members they have lost instead of how many they have gained. New communities are following the practice of the Church of the Saviour, Washington, D. C., in periodically renewing their vows of membership. In this way membership is not determined arbitrarily and matter-of-factly, but through the very deliberate, voluntary commitment of those who are willing to buy into the group consensus of what they are about. Honest confrontation, talking through to a consensus, voluntary acceptance of such consensus, and an opportunity to participate in the continuing consensus-making process may increasingly become the style of witness and life together.

Contrary to the frequent assumption that discipline and mission are antithetical, they belong together. Discipline implies learning; it is training that corrects, molds, strengthens, or perfects. Mission points to a purpose and a goal. As discipline becomes legalistic when separated from its vision, so mission lacks dynamic when it lacks any concretion or shape in the life and witness of the community. Historically, from the Irish monks to the class meetings of Wesley, it has been the disciplined cadres that have had a powerful impact on culture. The caricature by Ernst Troeltsch and Max Weber of sects as withdrawn from culture can easily mislead. It is true that subsequent generations of sectarians have often withdrawn to safe conclaves as a result of severe persecution. But the first Anabaptists and Quakers, for example, were vigorous in their confrontation of society. While most of the Reformers felt that the Great Commission had been fulfilled by the early apostles, the Anabaptists firmly asserted that the command to baptize and preach in all the world was given to each Christian in his day. Thus their preachers were to be found in the heart of the major cities. The Anabaptists sought disputations with other representatives of the Reformation in order to argue their case. The movement was prevented from mushrooming throughout all of Europe only by severe persecution. In the sense of denoting narrow particularity, the word "sectarian" is more accurately applied to those who wedded the Reformation to the faith of the magistrate than to those who universalized the Great Commission and preached love for all men, even for one's enemies.

THE PROPHETIC COMMUNITY

Such disciplined countercommunities in mission point to a style of radical witness, nonconformity, and prophetic action. Basic to the stance of the early Anabaptists was the belief that the proclamation of love and justice for the world must come from a brotherhood that knows genuine charity and equitable sharing in its own life. Their view of the Lord's Supper and baptism witnessed to this belief. Anabaptists such as Menno Simons and Peter Rideman felt that it was idolatrous to argue over the exact location of Christ in the host. They placed his real presence in the body of believers. According to Rideman the meaning of the Lord's Supper is that it is "a sign of the community of his body, in that each and every member thereby declareth himself to be of one mind, heart, and spirit with Christ."[13]

Anabaptist themes relating to baptism, such as preparing for personal testimony, following the example of Christ's baptism, and proclaiming the gospel to all the world, point to ordination as a basic theological ingredient in this act. This view agrees with Markus Barth's interpretation of baptism in the New Testament. Barth denies that baptism is a salvation rite or an initiation into a mystery cult. Rather, it is a stepping into ministry, a unique public beginning, a pledge to join the ministry of witnesses.[14] If 1 Peter is indeed a sermon to the newly baptized, it is significant that they are addressed as the "royal priesthood." The radical application of this view to our day would identify baptism less with membership in heaven or with a group of saints than with public ministry and prophetic witness. The paradigmatic baptism of Jesus as the time of entering public ministry would point to being saved from preoccupation with self to service for others.

Prophetic communities often develop counter life styles as an integral part of their witness. It is interesting to compare some of the nonconformity in current subcultures with the nonconformity of historic radical religious communities. An obvious example is dress. Religious radicals such as the Anabaptists and the Quakers eventually wore distinctive costumes. This mark of nonconformity symbolized simplicity of life and the priesthood of all believers (as the costume was not limited to clergymen), and publicly identified the wearer with a particular cause, such as pacifism. How ironic it is that some of the descendants of these nonconformists, who have gradually gained respectability, now plead with their youth to dress like others. These youth have identified with their subcultures as a way to express their nonconformity with the hypocrisy, militarism, materialism, and racism of their elders. Even their sloppiness and uncouth appearance, so offensive to many, serves as a sign denouncing all clean, respectable citizens who profit from the napalming and killing of others. Their style of dress offers a prophetic judgment not unlike the Woes pronounced by Jesus on those who were like white tombstones on the outside but full of dead men's bones (Matt. 23:27).

As with the Old Testament prophets, dramatic signs have frequently appeared as an element in the witness of religious radicals. The first congregation of Anabaptists near Zurich, Switzerland, took to the streets of that city in June of 1525. Men, women, and children wearing willow twigs or ropes instead of belts cried in loud voices for repentance. The early Quakers disrupted church services, confronted the powerful, and preached on hills and in jails of "the lamb's war" of John's Revelation. At the time of Cromwell in seventeenth-century England, the Diggers attempted to carve out a people's park or farm in an effort to convert idle land for profitable use by a religious communistic brotherhood. Prophetic and dramatic acts are appearing today in the form of guerrilla theater, marches, and street preaching.

THE ESCHATOLOGICAL COMMUNITY

Above all, the prophetic community must be a community of hope. Because of their embarrassment over the chiliasm of some of the Radical Reformers, some Anabaptist scholars have minimized the radical eschatology prevalent in large segments of the movement. Now they are perhaps becoming more receptive, as Carl Braaten notes in his recent book: "A new focus on eschatology will stir up old and faded memories about eschatological radicals whose writings were suppressed by the official orthodoxies of their time. Some back payments on accounts long overdue may be in order."[15] In a *Christian Century* article, Vernard Eller identifies the phenomenon he calls Protestant radicalism as primarily eschatological witness in the world. The radical churches, according to Eller, are those which have seen themselves from an eschatological perspective.[16] The apocalyptic feelings of some of the Anabaptists were shared by the Reformers. Luther, for example, was quite certain that the world would end in February, 1524. Since the Reformers identified the millennium with the Christianization of the Roman Empire, however, John Howard Yoder maintains that it was only with the Anabaptists that eschatology took on contemporary historical relevance: "The Anabaptists revived the two-aeon doctrine of the New Testament through their discovery that the 'world' is not simply an amorphous conglomerate of evil impulses but a structured reality taking concrete form in the demonic dimensions of economic and political life."[17] According to their faith, the most effective way to serve the old aeon, the world, is to live in the new aeon, the kingdom. Though some interpreted the various Christic schemes more literally than others, and though they differed in eschatological perspectives, the Radical Reformers all espoused an eschatological ethic. The way of the future kingdom was to be lived in the present. It was such an ethic of promise that served as the foundation for the pacifist witness of most Anabaptists. It is well summarized by Gordon Kaufman:

> Nonresistance is not based on any pragmatic conviction that it will

win the war or melt the hearts of the enemy or anything else of that sort; it is based on the eschatological conviction at the very heart of the Christian faith that the future is in Jesus Christ; and that therefore we can accept whatever that future might bring without regard for ourselves, even though it brings a cross.[18]

Because of the built-in tension in an eschatological view between the "now" and the "not yet," the Anabaptists identified with a particular cluster of New Testament terms used to describe the people of God—namely, "pilgrims," "sojourners," "strangers," and "aliens." Since society is fallen or sick, the Christian cannot feel at home. Therefore he espouses a citizenship in the kingdom which is not yet of this world but which should begin to break into the world. The posture of the pilgrim is not so much of one who is running away from the world as of one who has a transcendent vision of what the world might become. The metaphors of strangers and aliens point to the inevitable suffering of the pilgrim people.

Another important image appropriated from the Bible to describe the eschatological community has been that of firstfruits or earnest. The members of the community are the firstfruits pointing to the coming harvest. The community is the down payment guaranteeing that the rest of creation will be purchased. The sharp church-world dualism objectionable in some Anabaptist forms becomes more palatable in an eschatological perspective viewing the church as that part of the world where small beginnings are made to make visible what God intends for all humanity.

All the biblical metaphors imply a gathered community *in* the world but not *of* it. Today, as then, there can be no genuine revolutionary consciousness or activity apart from a base in a prophetic community of hope. The biblical images also point to the nonconformist, unpopular, minority nature of radical Christian communities. Because of the necessity of suffering, of nonconformity, of a loving life style, it may be that only a few will find their way to revolutionary Christian communities.

CHAPTER III

Beyond the Death of God

Since the startling death-of-God movement co-opted the label "radical" for itself, we must examine certain aspects of this phenomenon to clarify our understanding of genuine radical theology. In spite of the ardent efforts to pronounce in turn a death sentence on this neo-atheistic movement, following its crescendo and diminuendo in the sixties, the issues raised continue to impinge on current theologizing. Here we will examine some truly radical accents along with some elements I think are less than radical, given our dual perspective of radical as returning to the roots and as challenging the status quo. Our primary concern will then be to try to move beyond the usual debate and to develop leads posited by the death-of-God theologians concerning the meaning of freedom.

BROTHER ATHEIST

Christians should possess a built-in sense of charity toward atheists of every kind because atheism was one of the charges commonly leveled against the early Christian martyrs. The political and religious Establishment has often defamed as atheists those whose only crime was to deviate from the status quo. Martin Luther King, for example, found himself in a long succession of alleged Christian heretics when he was labeled a "Communist" and "atheist" by his detractors. Christendom has often downed alleged atheists by aligning with brutal forces and faithless paranoic fear. The unfortunate story of the Crusades and the sad spectacle of the Inquisition are all too representative of a violation of what we have seen as one of the fundamental tenets of the Radical Reformers, namely that there should be no official coercion in matters of religious belief and practice. Whereas many radicals of the past have been called atheists when in reality they considered themselves orthodox believers, the death-of-God radicals have wanted to be identified with atheism even when others were judging them to be theists. This theism has been felt because the death-of-God theologians have contended that God once lived and Thomas J. J. Altizer has evangelistically espoused a mysticism pregnant with a new immanence of God.

How the radical Christian should react to those who pronounce God's death is more than an academic question. Large segments of the Peace and Freedom Movement, young idealistic leftists, black and third-world revolutionaries, and humanist Marxists working for justice and equality reject the philosophical and theological forms of theism they have experienced. Because of the power of Marxism in much of the world and the growing identification of many youth with Marxian motifs, it may be helpful to listen to a Christian who has encountered atheism in the eastern European socialist matrix. Jan Lochman, only recently appointed to a chair of theology at Basel following a distinguished career as a leading Czech churchman and theologian, offers instructive guidelines for a "Gospel For Atheists."[1]

First, the encounter of Christians with atheists must proceed in the spirit of the gospel, which is the spirit of freedom. Lochman declares that "The gospel is the message of the sovereign freedom of God, and there is included in that the freedom of the Christian man."[2] This rules out mythologizing the adversary as a demon who must either be kept out through a ghetto psychology or driven out in a crusade.

Second, this spirit of freedom and openness, according to Lochman, will mean that the dialogue should not remain exclusively at the level of ideology. Ideology is important, and ideological discussion must be pursued, but man is more than his ideology. When the Christian focuses on Communist ideology instead of the man, the gospel itself becomes ideologized and is turned into a counter-ideology. "The really new possibility and the one thing which we really owe to the atheist," Lochman affirms, "is the message about the sovereign love of Christ. That love shatters every ideological barrier in order to seek and to find man: to seek and to find the Christian and the heathen, the pious and the worldly, the theist and the atheist."[3]

Lochman's third guideline calls for an attitude of meeting others in the way of pro-existence, being *for* others instead of living in an attitude of self-righteousness. Since atheism is often a response to the historical unfaithfulness of Christians and the support of injustice by the church, the Christian must approach these prophetic critics in the spirit of penitence and of solidarity with their humanistic concerns.

In the West such approaches to atheism are judged by some to illustrate the too easy submission of Christians in Communist countries. Most such accusations, however, have been made by Christians who themselves seem to have compromised their faith through a too easy harmonization of Christianity with capitalist ideology and practice. Actually, Lochman's essay is quite confrontative as he poses questions which from the perspective of the gospel must be put to atheistic humanism. For example, he raises the issue of "whether the way of atheism does not threaten the very thing it seeks to preserve, that complete undiminished humanity of man."[4]

The intriguing nature of the dialogue initiated by such Christians as Lochman and Josef Hromadka and such Marxists as Roger Garaudy and Ernst Bloch is indicated in an incident reported by Jürgen Moltmann. While journeying to Prague, Moltmann read a long report in *Time* on the death-of-God movement in the United States. Upon arriving at his destination, he was given a series of articles written by a *Marxist* philosopher, Gardavsky, on Jacob, Jesus, Paul, and Augustine entitled: "Buh neni zcela mrtev" ("God Is Not Quite Dead").[5] Where they have occurred such mixture and rapprochement have been characterized by the increased activity of Christians in relating the gospel to the present-day struggle for freedom and justice at the same time Marxists have demonstrated a fresh openness to the possibilities of transcendence within a humanist framework.

Because of the cross-fertilization of the Christian with many other strands of radicalism in the Peace and Freedom Movement, it may be helpful to consider the stance vis-à-vis Christianity and secularism of a man who struggled against Nazism. In his *Ethics* Dietrich Bonhoeffer provides an exegesis of the "with me" and "against us" biblical texts which may become increasingly relevant in our post-Constantinian situation. His concrete experience in the Confessing Church, which was forced to confess its faith without hedging in the face of the Nazi regime, led him and his colleagues to feel that the greatest of all dangers threatening the church was the neutrality of large numbers of Christians. Thus Bonhoeffer reports that they came to know the truth of Jesus' saying in Matthew 12:30: "He who is not with me is against me, and he who does not gather with me scatters."[6] Bonhoeffer flirted with radical church possibilities and experiments, and his stance approximated to some degree that which has currently evolved in disciplined prophetic countercommunities.

But in his freedom struggle Bonhoeffer also had many associations with atheists, humanists, Communists, and others outside the church. These comrades were passionately concerned about "injured justice, oppressed truth, vilified humanity, and violated freedom."[7] In his alliance with these men, Bonhoeffer experienced the truth of Jesus' other saying in Mark 9:40: "For he that is not against us is for us." Bonhoeffer says: "The particular concrete instance to which this saying refers, is the case of a man who, without himself being a disciple or follower, nevertheless casts out devils in the name of Jesus."[8]

The attitudes expressed in these two sayings of Jesus appear contradictory, but Bonhoeffer came to realize that the two claims, "the claim to exclusiveness and the claim to totality," belong together. "The more exclusively we acknowledge and confess Christ as our Lord," Bonhoeffer wrote, "the more fully the wide range of His dominion will be disclosed to us."[9] Prophetic voices today are calling for this same cutting exclusiveness for the sake of the inclusiveness of the gospel. For example, when churches attempt to become more inclusive in their love by expressing concern for oppressed peoples, they may lose members who worship a tribal god. Christian radicals may receive their dynamic in the life of a disciplined committed community; but at the same time, their ecumenicity (the word literally refers to the relationship of the church to the entire world) will be expressed in their sharing life with the movements for peace, freedom, and justice. The word "brother" is used in the Bible not only to greet a fellow Jew or Christian, but is universalized in the twenty-fifth chapter of Matthew to include all who belong to the community of lowliness and suffering. Jesus designated as "my brethren" (vs. 40) the hungry, the thirsty, the sick, the naked, and those in prison.

TRULY RADICAL

We have seen that atheism has often sprung from a genuine insight into what faith in God *should* mean but does not in the lives of so-called Christians. The failure of God's people to translate creed into life has resulted in the rejection of the static God of the status quo. Similarly, the death-of-God movement has represented a valid judgment on the faithlessness of Christendom. And since this judgment is valid, since the reality of God is in fact dead in the lives of millions of nominal Christians, the pronouncement of this posed a serious threat to all who were clinging to propositional statements about God's existence or nature. The radicalism of the movement consisted in its challenge to many to examine anew the roots of their faith.

In defining the God who is dead as the God of historic Christendom, Altizer was right in feeling that this negative proclamation could help pave the way for a new epiphany of faith. In rejecting the metaphysical superstructure erected by the Greek fathers, the death-of-God theologians abetted the recovery of the dynamic God of biblical faith. The dehellenization process has likewise been a part of the recovery of the apocalypticism of the early church, which is becoming increasingly meaningful to many today. Above all, this controversy has forced Christians to reexamine the nature of faith itself. In the Bible faith is not to be equated with sight. Paul testified that Christians only know in part, their knowledge is imperfect, and they only see as through a glass dimly (1 Cor. 13). In reality, there is no faith without an "in spite of," which is doubt. It is this radical "in spite of" which makes faith, faith. This interrelatedness between doubt and the venture of faith is evidenced in the New Testament witness "I believe, help my unbelief" (Mark 9:24).

The death-of-God theologians have frequently been commended for their exposé of attempted manipulations and false conceptions of God. If God's name is too holy to be pronounced in the Old Testament, the idea of being chummy with God that is typical of much popular religion in America is suspect. William Hamilton was led down the path to finally proclaiming God's death by a strong sense of identity with Bonhoeffer's critique of the *deus ex machina*, the god of the gaps, whom we call upon to meet our needs, solve our problems, and fill in the missing links of our knowledge. This movement has represented the most pungent of the many critiques of American cultists who have used God to achieve physical health, peace of mind, and worldly success.

Although we need to take the chief spokesmen for the Movement at face value in their claim to have pronounced God's death rather than having criticized false conceptions of God, their efforts have, nevertheless, provided the spadework to help unearth a fountain of interest in the problem of God. A succession of studies has emerged in which God-talk has come alive and meaningful in a new way. Such have been the fresh presentations of process philosophy and natural theology by such theologians as Schubert Ogden, John Cobb, and Langdon Gilkey. In *A Rumour of Angels,* Peter Berger, critic-turned-apologist, finds anthropological signals of transcendence in the human propensity for order, the playful elements in human culture, and Bloch's argument from hope.[10] Gordon Kaufman through his historicist perspective points to the possibility of meaningful God language without mythology by appropriating the analogy of personal relationships.[11]

The view of transcendence as openness to the future as articulated by a growing number of theologians of hope is well expressed by Richard Shaull: "The transcendent reality described in the biblical myths and images is not so much the God who stands above all human attainments, judging them and raising man to a higher order, but the God who goes ahead of us, opening the way for greater fulfillment on the road to the future."[12] The notion of God as the power of the future is coming to have more meaning for many than the idea of God as the "ground of being." It is this focus on the transcendence of the future which is making sense to atheist Marxist philosophers such as Roger Garaudy. In a real sense, the questions, criticisms, and discussion vitalized by the death-of-God debate have served as a catalyst for many fresh approaches to the possibilities of a new transcendence. The radical challenge to the old has helped bring into being exciting formulations of the new.

LESS THAN RADICAL

The chief problem with the death-of-God theology is not its offensive language, its near blasphemy. For its language poses no threat to those who experience the radical nature of the faith and to whom the bold announcements of God's death have simply made a valid judgment on the church's doctrine and life. The real problem with the movement has been that it too easily falls short of the prophetic mission it claims. Because its prophecy has been more stringently directed at the God of Christendom than at the gods of American culture, its radicalism has often been more alleged than real. In spite of the shock wave of public reaction, the death-of-God movement did not present as serious a threat to the basic institutions of American life as did the concurrent evangelical and nonviolent activity of Martin Luther King. One of the underlying motivations of these theologians seemed to be a desire to be contemporary. They wished to make faith palatable to modern man and to "do theology" in the light of what has happened to the consciousness of twentieth-century man.

In concentrating on the experience of modern man, the death-of-God radicals adopted what I shall call a *nonreligious a priori*. Karl Barth had attacked the *religious a priori* (the assumption that man is naturally religious) in order to emphasize the primacy of God's grace over man's religious quest. Dietrich Bonhoeffer had repudiated the notion of the *religious a priori* as a part of his debunking the notion that meeting man's need constitutes the essence of Christianity. William Hamilton followed Bonhoeffer's repudiation, but through introspective analysis and phenomenological study was led to a *nonreligious a priori*, the idea that men are basically nonreligious.

Paradoxically, the death-of-God theologians arrived at a *nonreligious a priori* by way of a religious one, for they declared that God had once lived. In this they were not atheists in the traditional sense. If God had never existed, their program of pronouncing his death would have been absurd. God once lived, however, and then died. His death is attributable to man and is datable. In their volume *Radical Theology and the Death of God*, Hamilton and Altizer traced the history of the divine dying, focusing primarily on nineteenth-century writings and ideas— those of William Blake, Hegel and the Hegelian Left, Darwinism and Nietzsche. They found the causes of the death "lying at the very center of vision and experience."[13] They quoted Zarathustra's oracle: "God is dead and we have killed him." Hamilton testified that for him the death of God occurred when, reflecting on the genocide of the Jews by Hitler, he became disenchanted with the problem-solving, need-fulfilling God. Thus God's death occurs in the consciousness of nineteeth- and twentieth-century men. Thomas Merton's critique may be too harsh and unfair, but it does help reveal a possible credibility gap in any discovery of the *nonreligious a priori:* "To say that modern man cannot believe in God because God is unbelievable to modern man and to conclude that any modern man who believes in God is therefore faking: this is not only questionable logic but it seems to me to savor a little of the same bad faith of which it accuses the believer."[14]

With the growing emphasis on the *historical a priori*, which focuses both on the historic rootage of the faith and on a theology of hope, the Barthian prejudice against anthropocentrism is revived in a different way. The current theological shift is from an emphasis on man's limits and man's anxiety to man's responsibility, from a preoccupation with man's nature to a concentration on his moving forward through history, from theological anthropology to theological messianism. This analysis places the so-called radical theologians of God's death among the last representatives of the more personal trend in theology. This means that radicalism as espoused here will be more concerned about what it was that enabled the early Christians to turn the world upside down than with building bridges to secular philosophies. The neo-atheist radical is concerned to be "with it" in our modern age. The more biblically oriented radical is more likely to challenge such accommodations. The death-of-God radical challenged Christendom in the name of modernity; the type of radical I wish to delineate in this book challenges society in the name of the coming kingdom. The neo-atheist radical derived his position from an analysis of man as he is; the more contemporary radical bases his faith on the hope of the coming of the new humanity.

The same movement from either a *religious* or *nonreligious a priori* to a *historical a priori* can be seen in relation to the question of theodicy. The questioning of the love and power of God in relation to pain and suffering often reappears in a new form. A political and social dimension is added to the plight of the Jobs of history. The question of social justice has become the updated form of the theodicy problem. Both the Jewish theologian Richard Rubenstein and William Hamilton rejected the concept of the faithful God of Israel in reflecting on the genocide of the Jewish people under Hitler. How can one extol God's faithfulness in the face of the gas ovens of the concentration camps? Since both of these theologians retained their faith in man, it is relevant to pose a counter question for them. If one rejects the notion of God's providence because of the horrible experiences of Auschwitz, how can one continue to believe in man? Why do not such manifestations of man's gross inhumanity to his fellow man undercut one's faith in man as well as his faith in God? The radical death-of-God theologians call for our being with Jesus in his stance for others. But can men who have been so brutally sadistic become transformed into men for others? This vision involving a new optimism about man may in reality imply an openness to the transcendent possibilities of change in the future, a notion traditionally expressed in God-talk.

RADICAL FREEDOM

It is on the subject of freedom that radicals in the Peace and Freedom Movement may have a fruitful dialogue with the death-of-God radicals. For it may be in considering the positive counterpoint of the negative proclamation of God's death that one can move beyond the usual debate. Altizer's definition of God as Jesus prompted the parody: "There is no God and Jesus is his son." Having lost faith and hope, Hamilton proposed that the thing left for the theologian was love and the place for him to stand was with Jesus, one who was free to be the man for others. Paul Van Buren, who was often identified as a reluctant member of the neo-atheist trinity, focused on the contagious freedom of Jesus. His important book *The Secular Meaning of the Gospel* attempted to develop Christian doctrines without God-language as an exercise in meeting the linguistic standards of analytic philosophers.[15] Fundamental to the Christian perspective or *blik* is the freedom of Jesus from self and his freedom to be for others. As defined by Van Buren, the resurrection occurred when the disciples adopted this *blik* for themselves; conversion occurs when one is grasped by this perspective sufficiently to be free to give himself for his neighbor. Although there are limitations to such a representation of Jesus divorced from his theistic and eschatological framework, this interpretation of freedom may prove to be the most radical contribution of the death-of-God movement.

FREEDOM FROM

Before developing this radical theme of freedom *for*, it may be helpful to consider some more popular appeals for freedom *from*. The current youthful rebellion demands that the word "freedom," which is used so loosely in contemporary life, be given some substance. Herbert Marcuse is right in charging that the analytic philosophers are largely therapists in their preoccupation with defining the terms used in the noncontroversial manipulated order rather than in adopting the critical stance of traditional philosophy.[16] For example, why have not linguistic philosophers attacked more vigorously such perversions of language as the commonplace use of "free world" to designate such political entities as fascist Spain, right-wing dictatorships in South America, and corrupt, oppressive regimes in southeast Asia? In a day of big government, big business, big armies, and bigger and bigger universities, there is an increasing desire to be free from the domination and control of others. In reaction to the authoritarianism of a warfare state and the depersonalization of a technological society, the alienated generation appropriated the existentialist declaration of freedom in the face of many kinds of psychological, economic, sociological, theological, and historical determinism. We are living in a time when civil liberties and the freedom to dissent from prevailing cultural gods are preserved only through struggle and at great cost.

The Marxist coupling of equality with freedom points to the necessity of witnessing also for freedom *from* the tyranny of economic exploitation and powerful vested interests. Whereas we fear the denial of personal freedom at the hands of large collectivities, the Russian fears a laissez-faire individualism which if not controlled runs roughshod over the rights of others. Our concern is for civil liberties for the individual—the freedom to speak, to assemble, and to protest. The Russian's concern is for a freedom of opportunity that can be gained only through equality and justice. If one man is permitted to own ten houses, the Russian points out, this means that nine men are denied the chance to own any. Our faith centers on the moral individual, with a built-in suspicion that society is immoral. The socialist's faith in society's protection of equality makes him suspicious of the egoism of individual man.

Analyzing the difference between Western and Eastern freedom, a German friend of mine observed that freedom in America has been characterized by the cherished personal liberty to express and hold dissident viewpoints. (He was, however, quite shocked to discover that we do not possess this freedom to the degree he had anticipated. He observed a businessman who because of community pressures was not free to express his views on the war in Viet Nam, high school students who were not free to distribute their underground paper, and teenagers who were not always free to wear their hair the way they wished in public schools.) In distinction from the type of personal freedom featured in the West, he pointed to the greater freedom to develop according to one's ability that, he felt, existed in the East. For example, the Soviet Union offers greater educational equality than does America, where there is generally a great discrepancy between the quality of education in the suburbs and that in the inner city. Our best dream should envision a society in which equal opportunity and justice are combined with individual liberties.

There are definite biblical and theological themes buttressing the secular quest for freedom *from*. First, there are those motifs pointing to freedom as freedom from law, the past—especially the oppressive and authoritarian past. One theologian who has defined freedom as release from such personal slavery is Rudolph Bultmann. Identifying Heidegger's unauthentic existence with Paul's natural man, Bultmann defines such existence as a state in which the decisions are made for the self by the collective mass of mankind. True freedom comes by being met with a word of forgiveness and acceptance. Man is freed for commitment and decision when delivered from past hang-ups and controls.

This freedom from the past is expressed in the Old Testament, where the related word for freedom is *shintah* or "release." Deuteronomy 15 states that such a release from inequities should be granted at the end of every seven years. Every creditor should release what has been loaned to his neighbor, and every brother who has been sold should be freed. Release or freedom is this: "You shall open wide your hand to your brother, to the needy and to the poor, in the land" (15:11). The Sabbatical Year and the Year of Jubilee as outlined in Leviticus 25 point to a new equalitarian beginning in which all of the inequities and oppressions of the past are righted. As the Pauline message has been interpreted to point to freedom from law and sin, so a Johannine framework will point more to freedom from fate and meaninglessness. Victor Frankl has reported that the only people whose personal dignity could survive the Nazi death camps were those who knew purpose, meaning, and hope beyond self. A real power of the Judeo-Christian tradition has been its offer of meaning and purpose through tasks to be accomplished and a witness to be made to a coming kingdom.

Similarly, the Bible offers a message of freedom from worshipping nature. Writing in Galatians 4:3 that "we were slaves to the elemental spirits of the universe," Paul proclaims the Christian's freedom from nature in Colossians 2:20. Because the true representation or spirit of God was placed in a person, the Christian revolution freed man from being subject to trees, stones, mountains, or other objects inhabited by spirits. Freed thus from the power of animism, the early Christians helped pave the way, philosophically, for the advent of modern science. For when man no longer worshipped material objects, he was free to manipulate them. Unfortunately, the freedom to manipulate has evolved into a propensity to rape. This wanton exploitation of nature has backfired in a threat to man's own existence, as the stockpiles of bombs and military hardware and the pollution of our water, soil,

55

and atmosphere make painfully obvious. Such a situation does not call for a return to an idolatry of nature but for a theology of reverent and Franciscan respect for brother creatures and creation.

In a real sense the Bible also freed men from the ultimate authority of the state. The early Christians demythologized the cult of Caesar because they knew another Lord. It is true that one cannot find a strong case for anarchy in the biblical materials. Passages such as Romans 13 suggest that the principle of government is valid and that we are to be subject to the higher authorities wherever possible. But it is clear in the light of the example of Paul and others that in any conflict of allegiance the Christian must obey God rather than man. Romans 13 must be considered with Revelation 13 where the state is pictured as a beast when it usurps the authority that belongs to God alone. An excellent summary statement of freedom *from* is that of Paul in his letter to the Galatians (5:1): "Plant your feet firmly therefore within the freedom that Christ has won for us, and do not let yourselves be caught again in the shackles of slavery" (Phillips translation).

FREEDOM FOR

For the death-of-God theologians a valid freedom *from* must also embody a freedom *for.* The freedom *from* a belief in the God of Christendom should lead to a freedom to be a man *for* others. Such radicalization also means that freedom *from* authoritarianism must be accompanied by freedom *for* responsible participation in the decisions which bear on one's existence. Freedom *from* jingoistic adulation of the state should signal freedom *for* humanity.

This analysis of being a free man *from* oppression and a free man *for* others is not, of course, novel. Paul wrote of his missionary strategy: "For though I am free from all men, I have made myself a slave to all, that I might win the more" (1 Cor. 9:19). And in his classic tract *On Christian Liberty* Luther defined both freedom *from* and freedom *for:* "A Christian man is the most free lord of all, and subject to none; a Christian man is the most dutiful servant of all, and subject to everyone." In this same Lutheran vein, Bonhoeffer related freedom to the Christian view of the reality of God. This may in part have been what he had in mind when he criticized Karl Barth's "positivism of revelation." Barth had stressed God's sovereign freedom from all man's rationalizations, projections, and conceptions. Against all efforts to make God a captive of the machinations of man, the Barthians cried, "Let God be God." For God, they stressed, is not the static object of our thoughts but a living subject. Central to the meaning of revelation was the truth that God was free *from* man. Bonhoeffer essentially accepted this Barthian analysis but believed that it lacked a crucial dimension. At the heart of the biblical message, he felt, was the news of Immanuel, God with us. Though it may be a good philosophical axiom to state that God was free *from* man, the New Testament message reflects on the experience that God was free *for* man.[17]

Obviously the death-of-God theologians did not follow Bonhoeffer in placing their view of freedom *for* in the context of theism. Neither did they, however, place their analysis of the man for others in a psychological or sociological framework. Rather, their supreme paradigm was the contagious freedom of Jesus. This christological center has caused many to find in their view an implicit doctrine of redemption. Thomas Ogletree, for example, thinks that Hamilton's effort to engage in theological discourse without referring to God confirms that the substance of "Godtalk" is present whether explicitly acknowledged or not. Observing that we often find the secular man self-centered and preoccupied with his own goals, Ogletree asks:

> How does this self-interested man come to find himself alongside his neighbor in love? Clearly some sort of redemptive process is involved which frees man from the drive to grasp life for himself and for the possibility of giving himself to his neighbor. Yet it is precisely such a redemptive process that has been traditionally understood as the work of God in and through the announcement and personal appropriation in faith of Jesus Christ.[18]

Whether one attributes it to love, a miracle, or God, the wonder of the man for others, wherever he appears, provides us, I think, with an excuse to seek some additional theological and biblical props.

First, we can speak of freedom for discipleship. Since discipleship implies following, we have introduced here the Christian paradox that true freedom may come through obedience. This paradox is to be found in Paul's proclamation to the Christians at Rome that though they have "been set free from sin, [they] have become slaves of righteousness" (Rom. 6:18). This is the claim that when one becomes free from his own self-centeredness, his own personal hang-ups, he is free to be obedient to the command to love others.

Another way of speaking of this same Christian theme is to speak of freedom in terms of response. When a man is freed from preoccupation with himself and his sins by being accepted and loved, then he is free to love someone else. The freedom to love comes in response to being loved. And love has often come through those who have been penetrated by the stream of love flowing from the man who died on the cross. To be free is to somehow want to do what one ought to do. It is to desire that which fits into the movement toward the coming of the kingdom of righteousness and justice. If one is lost in the forest, there are many possibilities. One can be free to go in any direction and still be lost. True freedom consists in discerning the direction which leads out of the forest and acting on the basis of this belief.

Such freedom for discipleship may be seen in the historic *kenotic* motif which affirms a Jesus who "though he was in the form of God, did not count equality with God a thing to be grasped, but emptied himself, taking the form of a servant, being born in the likeness of men" (Phil. 2:5-7). Traditionally it has been emphasized that Jesus emptied himself of divine attributes to become a man like us. But an intriguing interpretation is that Jesus emptied himself of the human propensity to put one's self at the center of existence and thus take the place of God. In this way he became open so that God could use him to be the man for others.

A second theological *for* which is meaningful for contemporary radicals is the freedom for community. My colleague Graydon Snyder, a New Testament scholar, points out that the Christians at Corinth and Thessalonica took Paul's message of Christian freedom the wrong way. They felt they were free from the concerns of the community, free to eat any kind of meat without regard to the opinions of others, free to go to law in secular courts, free to speak in tongues even if others could not understand, free to uncover their heads even if this proved to be scandalous, and free not to work because they expected an imminent eschaton. In each case Paul needed to correct the false view that one is entirely free from the concerns of others. The biblical view is that we are genuine persons only in community. Man can know his real "I" only as that "I" comes into relation with the "Thou" of others. Real community requires the freedom of each person; the freedom of each person is possible only in loving relationships with others. The dialectic of this truth was expressed by Paul as the conclusion to his discussion of circumcision: "For you were called to freedom, brethren; only do not use your freedom as an opportunity for the flesh [meaning for Paul life lived out of proper relationship with others and God], but through love be servants of one another" (Gal. 5:13).

A third freedom offered by a release from forced faith, legalistic law, and personal pride is freedom for the future. A dynamic hope in the coming of the kingdom frees one *from* the fatalism of accepting the world as it is and *for* life as it should be. Because of his faith in the victorious nature of the eschaton, the Christian is free to play heaven on this dirty earth. Such faith eliminates the age-old problem of what might be called the zero sum theory of freedom. Such a view assumes that either there is a God who is in control and therefore man cannot be free, or man is free and there cannot be a God. What is granted to God must be taken away from man, and what is granted to man must be taken away from God. Moltmann feels that it is in this vein that Prometheus has become the philosophical saint of Marxism, for this ancient hero was the symbol of man's freedom over against the gods. Contrary to this view, Moltmann presents the view of freedom found in the biblical narrative:

> In the Old Testament, however, things are different. Yahweh is here the God who leads his people out of the house of bondage. Thus he is the God of freedom, the God "ahead of us." One acquires social, political, and world-surpassing freedom from God, not against him.[19]

In all of the talk about freedom today by young radicals, old conservatives, and middle-aged politicians, the possibilities offered by a belief in freedom *for* are often ignored. Helmut Gollwitzer in his book *The Demands of Freedom* recognizes our predicament.[20] Having spent time in Soviet prisons, this German theologian and preacher cannot be accused of naiveté about the pitfalls of Communist states. Nevertheless, he questions from a theological perspective our easy references to "the free West" and "the totalitarian East." Much of Western opposition to Communism arises, he is convinced, from a basic fear of losing property and a high standard of living and springs more from a slavery to self-centeredness than from a genuine Christian understanding of freedom. And while Gollwitzer would agree that no people have a monopoly on Christian freedom, he observes that in losing their preoccupation with institutional security some people behind the iron curtain have been freed to become in a truer sense men for others.

Dietrich Bonhoeffer made a profound theological distinction between costly and cheap grace. Cheap grace preaches forgiveness without requiring repentance. Costly grace requires repentance, a change of life, and discipleship.[21] The same distinction applies to freedom. Cheap freedom is freedom *from* the law without a freedom *from* sin. Costly freedom is freedom *from* sin so that one might be a slave to righteousness. Or we can state the distinction in less theological language. Cheap freedom is freedom *from* the authority of others without freedom *from* basic self-centeredness.

Costly freedom is freedom *from* basic self-centeredness, so that one is free *for* others. The death-of-God theologians focused on costly freedom. And such freedom is truly radical in challenging our usual understandings of freedom and in plumbing the depths of our faith.

CHAPTER IV

Radical Faith and the New Left

In comparing the themes of the theological left with political expressions of the new radicalism, my point of reference will be primarily the phenomenon known as the New Left. Evolving in this country from the demand of four students for a cup of coffee in North Carolina in 1960 and the Port Huron statement of the Students for Democratic Society in 1962, the New Left revolution in its broader manifestations includes the struggles and new identity of Blacks in America, the revolutionary ferment and heroes of the so-called third world, the growing anti-war and peace movement, and the student disaffection with bureaucratic and totalitarian attitudes whether found in government or university.

As "radical theology" is a label for shifting moods rather than any systematic proposal, the New Left has encompassed a plurality of groups and a wide umbrella of views and activity. In fact such pluralism is welcomed rather than feared. If freedom from the manipulation of any "system" is desired, great variations in ideology and style are beneficial. And if "your thing" needs to be done, then the multiplicity of organizational efforts is not to be deplored. In the struggles for human freedom and a peaceful world, the more cadres "doing their thing" the better. The idea of a Movement directed by an elite of international conspirators is a ludicrous caricature to any who have been a part of the chaotic and fragmented life of the New Left. Nevertheless, there have emerged common concerns and purposes which have frequently created bonds of unity between radicalized liberals and alienated youth, idealistic youth and black freedom leaders, radical churchmen and agnostic humanists, white niggers (hippies, Yippies) and radical theologians.

That the New Left is to be distinguished from the Old Left is illustrated by the fact that many young radicals have more in common with each other than with the regimes of their own countries. Whereas the Old Left politicized on the basis of the cleavage between the socialist East and the capitalist West, contemporary radicals have known common styles and resentments whether they have lived in Prague, Frankfurt, Madrid, Warsaw, or Berkeley. It is true that Marxist ideology has become increasingly significant in the nomenclature and analysis of the New Left, but this has come about primarily as a substantiation of present experiences rather than a "buying into" an old ideology. Some of the recurrent themes of the New Left have been a stress on freedom, participatory democracy through new institutions, and decentralization; a humanistic concern for the dispossessed; an attack on the hypocrisy of a sick society; a protest against war, racism, and economic exploitation; a quest for community; and an apocalyptic hope for a better world. The New Left has been more suspicious of ideology as such than has the Old Left. For them action is more important than theory.

Recognizing that "the times, they are a' changin'," the Movement is characterized by continuous transformations in its own life. Every few months bring new alignments, spokesmen, and attitudes—some of them good, some of them not. Unfortunately, some of the worst legacies of the Old Left are beginning to reappear in the New. For there has surfaced a "dogmatism, an obsession with factional purity, vilification of opponents, hysterical gestures of alienation, the cult of violence."[1]

"TELL IT LIKE IT IS"—UNITY OF WORD AND DEED

New Left activists have been characterized by an obsession for authenticity. Their passionate quest for personal integrity is not unlike the radical Christian's insistence on the unity of creed and life, word and deed, faith and works. Psychologist Kenneth Keniston's study, which finds young radicals to be committed youth, reveals a mood similar to a view of conversion which demands changed lives.[2] Unsatisfied until ideology has been translated into action, New Leftists have posed a real threat to society. The university tolerated free speech as long as students did not interfere with its military alliances, and society applauded brotherhood speeches as long as there were no concrete demands for justice.

This trait of authenticity came naturally from their personal and national histories. Many young radicals were nurtured in democratic homes where they were permitted to criticize their parents and where the best in the American heritage was revered. It has often been asserted that they believed what their high school commencement speakers said about freedom, equality, justice, human dignity, and world peace. The best educated of generations and the products of multi-media stimuli, the young radicals quickly sensed the discrepancy between America's ideals and her actions. When they learned of the record of American intervention in South America, the decades of inhumanity to Blacks, the corruption of power and militarism, they were morally outraged and ethically repulsed. They have waved American flags in demonstrations less out of sacrilege than out of the conviction that they are more American than the Establishment. Carl Oglesby at the November 27, 1965, march on Washington declared: "...Others will make of it that I sound mighty anti-American. To these I say: Don't blame me for that! Blame those who mouthed my liberal values and broke my American heart."[3]

Though flaunting traditional ethical values and respectable niceties of speech, dress, and behavior, some have nevertheless made attempts to identify with the roots of the Judeo-Christian heritage. Even the obscenities of today's youth represent a shift from the terms characteristic of their parents' profanity. The present obscenities often seem to attack the ethic of respectability. While many have repudiated religious faith as irrelevant and have even damned the institutional church for its false priorities and hypocrisy, there have been those who have seen their radical political stance as a natural outgrowth of their religious heritage. This sense of continuity with roots is revealed by the testimony of a young teenager who was threatening to become a draft resister. He related the intense conflict he had with his father, who was a veteran of the Korean war, and he told of the frustration of his mother who anxiously queried her neighbors, "What have we done wrong?" With tears in his eyes the long-haired lad exclaimed: "How can I convince her that it is not what she's done that's wrong, but it's what she has done that's right, that I don't want to kill other people."

The strong Woes hurled by Jesus at the hypocrites offer a paradigm of a fundamental mood of the New Left. Quite typical is this remark: "I was taught to sing, 'red and yellow, black and white, they are precious in God's sight,' only to discover that those who taught me this really didn't believe it!" In this way Jack Newfield has characterized the Left as the prophetic minority: "They came to cry out against the hypocrisy called Brotherhood week, assembly lines called colleges, manipulative hierarchies called corporations, conformity called status, lives of quiet desperation called success."[4] The young radicals have exposed the hypocritical sacred cows of American mythology. They have dug up the racist sentiments of Abraham Lincoln. With Stokely Carmichael they see in a simple statement like "Columbus discovered America" a racism which assumes that America, which was already inhabited, was really not discovered until the white man arrived. They would agree with Simon Bolivar, the father of South American revolutionaries, in his evaluation that "The United States appears to be destined by providence to plague America with misery in the name of liberty."[5] Worth Long's remark as a SNCC activist echo the sentiments of New Leftists: "We have found you out, fourfaced Americans, we have found you out."[6] For this reason radicals have been angered by the barrage of appeals to apply patience and nonviolence to the freedom struggle. These appeals come from those who are willing to use napalm and bombs, destroy crops, kill civilians, and create millions of refugees, all in the name of freedom. In his autobiographical account of his life as a young radical, Dotson Rader quotes his friend Rachael as saying, "Why do they have the right to use violence to maintain the System and we not have the right to use violence to change it?"[7]

It has been a surprise for many to discover that "liberal" is a bad word in the vocabulary of the New Left. For young radicals, many conservatives with basic honesty are more attractive than hypocritical liberals who mouth lofty sentiments but compromise with an oppressive Establishment. It has been the liberal and not the conservative, according to many radicals, who has guided America in its erroneous ways in our recent history. The liberal is the enemy. "The liberals got to be exposed. It's a liberal war in Vietnam. They're the warmongers, the power brokers, the enemy. . . ."[8]

Though in some areas of life youth today disavow the Puritanism bequeathed to them, their stance often does approach the New Testament insistence that the hearers of the Word must also be doers of the Word. The motto of the Diggers, "To be is to do," reminds us of the words of Jesus that the kingdom is not for those who say "Lord, Lord," but for those who do the will of the Father (Matt. 7:21). Jesus' critique of the respectable Pharisees and Sadducees of his day together with his acceptance of the unrespectable in his intimate circle is partially echoed in a remark by Steve Halliwell: "Until the concern with respectability is overcome in an individual's own life, he will be unable to create a politics that deals with the fact of how unrespectable the fabric of American life is at present."[9] In a recent confab designed to bridge the generation gap, a parent attacked the idealistic pacifism of one of the youth with the following realistic assessment: "Certainly, you realize that none of us live up to the ethical standards of Christianity. Why do you expect us to live up to this one?" To this the youthful idealist replied: "It is true that I fail to live by my ideals in many areas of my existence, but why should my hypocrisy in many things become a rationale for being hypocritical concerning this important issue?" Although the youth was admitting that he, like all men, was a sinner, he was not willing to argue that this fact should justify sinning all the more.

Such a plea for integrity, in reaction to the hypocrisy of society and the liberal politics of compromise, has raised anew the whole issue of strategy. In contradistinction to the official realism of the fifties in political science and Christian ethics, young radicals have been forced to consider the possibility of politics as the art of the *impossible*. Some are discovering the truth in Abbie Hoffman's declaration that "Political irrelevance is more effective than political relevance."[10] This bears similarities to a much older statement by Max Weber: "Certainly all historical experience confirms the truth that man would not have attained the possible unless time and again he had reached out for the impossible."[11] Many in the New Left do not ask whether an action is workable and likely to gain liberal support; rather the fundamental concern is with whether it is right.

Such a view can easily lead to a self-righteous perfectionism. On the other hand, it may reflect a chastened mood which moves from the stance "Because I am a sinner, I must compromise" to the confession "Because I compromise, I am a sinner." In this way the theme of relevance gives way to the theme of prophetic witness. Since it is no longer necessary to remain in good standing within the structures, one can really "tell it like it is." This mood has slightly radicalized my own casual conversations with seat companions in travel. I used to attempt to discern a person's bias and then attempt to moderate his views through subtle interrogation. Today I am more likely to tell him exactly how I stand on a major social issue. This most often evokes a similarly frank response, and then an interesting exchange begins in earnest. On the question of relevance we must heed the words of Bonhoeffer:

> But where the question of relevance becomes the theme of theology, we can be certain that the cause has already been betrayed and sold out....The intention should not be to justify Christianity in the present age, but justify the present age before the Christian message.[12]

NOT RADICAL ENOUGH

Though many New Leftists adamantly refuse to accommodate with evil within the System, they seem less adverse to appropriating the strategy of that System. I met with a group of bandaged McCarthy "kids" the morning after they had been beaten by the Chicago police during the historic Democratic National Convention. They articulated their anger: "We came to Chicago as pacifists. We leave as militants. Never again, will we allow policemen to beat us without responding with clubs of our own." A natural human response and one which is labeled as "being radicalized." It may, however, not be radical enough. It is possible that it represents a sellout to the System, for it adopts the very hatred and violence which radicals despise in the System. A more truly radical stance from a Christian perspective might be to refuse to become like the System which is opposed. This need not mean a meek acquiescence to all forms of violence. There is still room for the revolutionary pacifism of a David Dellinger and for a militancy against all forms of oppression without becoming like the oppressor. Neither does it necessarily mean that one will serve the interests of the rich by exhorting the poor and underprivileged to practice patience, meekness, and nonviolence to solve their problems. Rather the message of nonviolence should be preached to expose the institutionalized violence of the System. It should be preached to the police, national guard, and army troops as a challenge to cast out the beam from their own ethnic eye before beholding the splinters in the eyes of the dispossessed. As we shall discuss later, such an analysis is based on the assumption that the style of Jesus was even more revolutionary than that of the Zealots. True authenticity consists in trying to live the life one preaches.

"MAKE LOVE" — THE NEW HUMANITY

Carl Oglesby, one of the most articulate spokesmen for many young radicals, has stated that the purpose of the New Left is "to make love more possible."[13] While the radical Christian cannot sanction any rejection of the biblical view of sex, he can empathize with the current redefinition of pornography which views violence to human beings as more obscene than acts of physical love. Herbert Marcuse's perspective serves as a genuine judgment at this point:

> This society is obscene in producing and indecently exposing a stifling abundance of wares while depriving its victims abroad of the necessities of life; obscene in stuffing itself and its garbage cans while poisoning and burning the scarce foodstuffs in the fields of its aggression; . . . [what is] obscene is not the ritual of the Hippies but the declaration of a high dignitary of the Church that war is necessary for peace.[14]

Whereas the slogan "Make Love, Not War" often suggests only sexual love, Oglesby's version points to a broader humanistic concern which strives to eliminate those barriers in society which prevent genuine love and true community. This humanistic emphasis is reflected in the Port Huron statement, which declares that "men have unrealized potential for self-cultivation, self-direction, self-understanding, and creativity. . . . The goal of man and society should be human independence: a concern not with image or popularity but with finding a meaning in life that is personally authentic."[15] Such expressions explain why radicals so vigorously reject the vocations usually presented to educated youth. Typical replies from the Keniston study reveal the implicit humanism of the respondents. Reflecting on the relation of her graduate school experience to the future a girl affirmed: "I would like to teach people to be people—that is more important than writing a paper."[16] Similarly, a young man stated: "I'm not going to relate to machines, I'm not going to relate to books, I'm not going to relate to money. I am going to relate to people, on a very, very personal basis of service."[17]

The New Left has vigorously opposed the dehumanizing aspects of the System. Its attitude toward technology has been ambivalent. While on the one hand it sees technology as a means to liberate man through technological revolution, on the other hand it sees it as a tool of capitalist repression. This accounts for the popularity of Herbert Marcuse in the New Left. This elder philosopher defines as totalitarian not only "a terroristic political coordination of society, but also a non-terroristic economic-technical coordination which operates through the manipulation of needs by vested interests."[18] The rational character of this irrationality of industrial society claims the entire individual, according to Marcuse, and reduces man to a one-dimensional existence "in which ideas, aspirations, and objectives that, by their content, transcend the established universe of discourse and action are rejected or repelled."[19] For Marcuse, artists and traditional philosophers keep revolutionary possibilities alive when in their vision of something more they protest against what is.

The rejection of any form of servitude in which men exist as instruments or as things has led to the slogan that "human rights are more important than property rights." The order to shoot a boy running off with a TV set says that society is more interested in protecting property than in rehabilitating young life. Abbie Hoffman elucidates the same thought in a report of a YIP-In in Grand Central Station. Amidst the dancing and singing of thousands of people, a few climbed atop the information booth and began to pull at the hands of the clock. In the ensuing police attack, one boy was thrown through a glass door, breaking both hands, one of them permanently crippled. Abbie asks, "Which hands do you think the cops cared more about, the hands on the clock or Ron Shea's hands?"[20] Those youths who have gained most from an affluent society are often the very ones to discern most humanely the perils of prosperity. They see that prosperity often brings social indifference. They see that prosperity often corrupts values. The worth of a person is judged by the amount of money he controls.

Much in the humanism of the New Left is Christian. The affirmation that institutions should serve people, not people institutions, is but a restatement of Jesus' teaching about the institution of the Sabbath (Mark 2:27). Viewing the world through the eyes of the dispossessed, from the bottom up, is at one with the dominant prejudice of the biblical writers, who exalted the poor and condemned the rich. The desire to serve humanity rather than the mores of the Establishment clearly recalls Jesus' handling of the problem of authority: "You know that in the world the recognized rulers lord it over their subjects, and their great men make them feel the weight of authority. That is not the way with you; among you, whoever wants to be great must be your servant. . ." (Mark 10:42-43, New English Bible). The quest for true humanity jibes with a strong current of post-Bonhoefferian theology which has declared that God did not become man so that man might become divinized but so that man might become truly man or humanized. Current messianic interpretations of Jesus look to human history for the arrival of the new humanity and point to the shape of the new man in this history.

NOT RADICAL ENOUGH

The New Left has scintillated with brilliance in its diagnosis of the illness of modern society. Leftists have been charged, however, with failing to apply the same penetrating critique to themselves and their own actions. In this they may not be radical enough. Many in the Movement have failed to sufficiently consider the personal roots of sin, a teaching basic in the Judeo-Christian tradition. Structures are judged to be sick without an adequate diagnosis of how they got to be that way. This faith in moral man as opposed to immoral society can lead either to a black-white mentality which locates all evil outside oneself or to a similar mood which views man as basically good apart from his corruption by the forces of society. In some of its manifestations, therefore, the New Left has not escaped the naive humanism of the liberalism it attacks.

A young leftist organizer shared her convictions with the theological community to which I belong. She declared that the dispossessed are so badly exploited by the system that the basic goodness and great potentialities of the people cannot emerge. The common response of an academic theological group to such a presentation is to focus on its naiveté. But rather than attempting to puncture her idealism by emphasizing to her that men are sinners—in fact it seemed to me that her own life among the dispossessed may well have made her far more deeply aware of man's sinfulness than are many theological sophisticates—it would be better to present the christological basis that exists for such idealistic humanism. It is only when one has a high vision of what man should be that he can be impatient with the way man is. And it is only through a concrete experience with good men—or an "ideal" man—that we are convicted of how much less than really human most of us actually are. Through such a picture of the new humanity, one is freed to love man for what he might become instead of for what he is. It is this christological or theological basis for humanism that may claim to make possible a more radical humanism, one that enables us to love even the unlovely. This becomes possible when one is freed from the necessity of basing love on any idea of the innate or present loveliness or goodness of man. One no longer needs to base love on pragmatic results, but one loves because he recognizes God's love and intention for man.

R. W. Tucker notes that the quarrel of Christianity with other styles of humanism is a lover's quarrel. He points out that Christians must say both yes and no to Marxist humanism in its affirmation that "man is the measure of all things." Says Tucker, "Man is not the measure of all things. Sanctified man is the measure of all things." In spite of this difference, he does feel a common bond of unity:

> The real problem facing us all is not to oppose the humanist vision, in which man is the measure of all things, with the vision of a nobler world in which Christ is the measure of all things—but the prior difficulty of undoing a world in which things are the measure of man. Focussing on this, we are set free to put the so-called humanist challenge to Christianity in proper perspective, as a quarrel over

theory among people who are allies in practice. It is an important quarrel, but in many ways it need not be a divisive one.[21]

"TURN ON, TUNE IN, DROP OUT" — THE DREAM OF COMMUNITY

Turned off by the institutions bequeathed to them by previous generations, masses of our most interesting youth have heeded Timothy Leary's invitation to drop out from society and have tuned in on alternative life styles and communities. Though many of us in the Christian orbit might prefer that one be turned on by the power of the Christian good news rather than by an induced change in the body's chemistry, one must acknowledge the communal nature of the rituals and life styles of the radical youth culture. This sense of brotherhood and solidarity has been a mark of the Movement from its inception. The clasping of hands and swaying together while singing *"We* shall overcome" is indicative of the communal symbols and songs which have given a powerful sense of identity. All branches of the Movement have appropriated the use of "brother" and "sister" from the black community. A middle-aged participant in a mass demonstration shared with me her rationale and enthusiasm for her activity:

> The way we share food and greet one another I feel like we are together as one big happy family. In my neighborhood at home, I feel so lonely and different and sometimes wonder whether they may be right in judging me as a kook. But here, I am strengthened by the many who share my basic convictions, and I receive the shot in the arm to continue my activity for peace.

At one time the slogan of the drug culture seemed antithetical to the purposes of the activistic wing of the New Left. Since the activists were intent on prophetically confronting the System in order to change it, they looked upon the hippie types as cop-outs. On the other hand the dropouts, who were extremely skeptical about what might happen if the young activists succeeded in changing things, appealed to a different revolutionary idea—"do your thing as long as it doesn't interfere with anyone else's thing." Now, the sharp cleavage between the monastic and worldly Left no longer seems so certain and clear. Politically oriented resisters, forced by persecution to seek community, have been led to move beyond their negative reaction against the System to affirm life outside the System. At the same time, hippies became Yippees and spawned public festivals, guerrilla theater, and street confrontations. Although the tension between the two moods and wings is still present in the Movement, there has been a pronounced shift.

> A broad section of the Movement has gradually moved beyond a dependence on confrontation politics and traditional organizing techniques into the politics of alternative (not parallel) life-styles, and in so doing has developed, or is in the process of developing, an existential dialectic of revolution that differs with the thinking of the Old Left and breaks with much of the political orientation of the New Left as well. "One's life is one's only political instrument," Resistance organizer Dave Harris has said. "We must therefore develop a whole new way of life—a new mentality. And we must do it not by talking about it or leafleting but by living it."[22]

This feeling that dropping out can be a revolutionary act in itself has no doubt come from the deep sense of alienation that has been common to most members of the New Left. To frustration over the facelessness of modern life has been added the despair of powerlessness. Many youth in the Movement were initially political liberals trying to concretize their ideals by supporting liberal candidates and traditional ways of effecting change through the structures of society. Their radicalization came in confronting unkept promises, inflexible answers, denials of personal freedoms, and battered heads from the very institutions they had trusted. Working to help those at the bottom assume their right to make the decisions affecting their lives, young radicals became aware of their own disenfranchisement in political and university life. Old enough to become "fighting men" in the armed forces, they were regarded as adolescents by the educational system. Politically articulate and well-educated, they were not allowed to vote. According to Keniston's psychological analysis, we have a new class of people who are "psychological adults" but "sociological adolescents." They are those who have felt cut off from that which they basically love. The love-hate character of this alienation is expressed poignantly in the autobiographical account of Dotson Rader:

> For we were cut off . . . from the mainstream of American life. We were apart. . . . We were the Non-believers. Our failure was the fact that we continually sought community apart from ourselves, reprieving daily the American Dream that was sold to us long ago, unable to concede that the only possible community was in rebellion. And it was not simply political victimhood, but the pain of being outside. . . .[23]

With the alienated, who coming from democratic homes became disillusioned with democracy, we must include those who, coming from materialistic and emotionally unstable homes, were ready to lash out in adolescent rebellion. To complete the picture, we must add the crowd present in every era who gravitate toward any conflict.

Whatever the sources of the alienation, we have experienced an upsurge of alternative life styles. The common charge that nonconformists to our society become conformists to their own peers is valid in that the sense of alienation from one culture leads to a search for community with those who share the same alienation, problems, and convictions. As reported in the literature of the New Left, the varieties of life styles now appearing seem to be endless:

> Resistance brothers and sisters, like hippie families, have established communes in many cities; other families are buying land in rural areas to establish self-supporting homesteads that will be used as bases for activists. On the West Coast, resisters are talking of buying gas stations. Elsewhere, underground papers, music restaurants and other enterprises are run on a communal basis by people who have dropped out—or are beginning to drop out—from the established order.[24]

To this milieu can be added interesting combinations of contemporary life styles with the more traditionally religious. The

Young Friends of North America, for example, combine ingredients of the New Left with evangelical primitive Quakerism.

These attempts at authentic relationships in face-to-face communities recall the communities of the early church and all the communities in Christian history that have been modeled after them. The radical's disgust with American competitiveness and his espousal of cooperation is closer to the biblical teaching than many capitalistic versions of the Protestant work ethic. His belief in participatory democracy represents a continuity with the practice of consensus in left-wing religious communities and the universal priesthood of all believers that was a mark of primitive Christianity. His insistence on living a new life is akin to the Anabaptist insistence that brotherhood must be a reality in the church if the church is to prophetically proclaim brotherhood for the world. Though it would, of course, be mistaken to equate the outlook of the radical community with the vision of the Christian community, many Christians do feel that they can discern the Spirit moving in many of the manifestations of community in our time.

NOT RADICAL ENOUGH

There has been much speculation about the destiny of the young Leftists as they marry and find work. Some see them changing America as they assume roles of leadership in mainstream society. Others see them rapidly reverting to the value system they now reject as they settle in suburbia, climb the ladder of status and financial success, and wonder what they were really doing ten years ago occupying an administration building. As yet, the New Left has not found adequate ways for those who become associated with the conventional institutions of society to retain an active role in the Movement. "Until it solves the problem of continuity," writes critic Christopher Lasch, "the student Left will be a force for disruption but not, except indirectly, for major social change."[25] Lasch advocates that the young radicals join with radicalized liberals in creating a third-party movement which could form a base for long-term radical politics. As I have suggested, however, growing numbers would answer this problem of continuity with more permanent and inclusive life styles—whole communities and subcultures encompassing not only the political aspects of life, but economic, artistic, and psychological aspects as well. I share the conviction that something more radical than a third party is needed at this time in history; at the same time I share Lasch's fear that these alternative life styles may easily become apolitical.

Preserving current concerns through community life styles requires, from a Christian perspective, a sense of continuity with the past. I agree with Richard Shaull that there is a great need to appropriate in new ways the symbols and experience of revolutionary Christian communities in the past. This can teach the dangers of idolizing community at the expense of any awareness of transcendent judgment, purposes, and goals. Communes have all too often existed simply for themselves rather than for the sake of the revolutionary coming of the new humanity or the kingdom of God. Without a transcendent eschatological goal, the community can become ingrown. Without a strong sense of a transcendent power the life of the community can degenerate into a cultic worship of its own practices or its own charismatic leadership. A truly radical community will incorporate an authentic style which helps facilitate the unity of Word and deed, one which will foster not only a love for others within the community but a freedom for the community to exist for the sake of pointing to and participating in God's transformation of his world.

"THE WAR IS OVER" — CONVERSION AND HOPE

Phil Ochs' song and Phillips' translation of the Pauline eschatological proclamation of the proper relationship between different ethnic groups bear the same title (Eph. 2:17). "The War Is Over" asserts ultimate reality more than present fulfillment, whether speaking of the reconciliation between Jew and Gentile or the coming of peace between the nations. Yet in terms of personal decision or world brotherhood, the promise is not altogether future. It is very much present. The war *is* over. For it signals the beginning of the realization of ultimate reality in our present lives and situation. We can begin to live now as if the war is truly over.

I have listened to young political radicals speak of the necessity for radically changed lives. They have pronounced the death sentence on the old as a prelude to the birth of the new. Their impatient mood has demanded peace and justice *now*. In countering this call for immediate revolutionary change, I have often joined fellow churchmen with the caution: "Change does not come quickly, take it easy, do not rock the boat too strenuously, give the system a chance." Yet, reflecting on some of these debates between people inside and outside the church, I have often wondered which side was really more biblical. For the young radicals sound some biblical notes in taking the matter of change very seriously, in calling for the death of the old and the birth of the new.

In general, participants in the New Left have been characterized by deep personal commitment. Paul Potter's challenge has been echoed in many branches of the Movement: "By social movement I mean more than petitions and letters of protest; I mean people who are willing to change their lives, who are willing to challenge the system, to take the problem of change seriously."[26] This similarity to religious conversion was noted by Tom Bell in a letter to Staughton Lynd:

> The sessions in the student union are very much like revival services (even including some of the rhetoric at times). We have speeches, a collection for the anti-war office and on-the-spot conversions— signing pledges, plus a lot of personal witnesses.[27]

Demonstrations, confrontations, and other common actions have all been occasions for gaining new converts, changing perspectives, renewing commitment, and establishing a strong sense of comradeship.

The powerful dynamic of personal commitment has resulted, in part, from the radicals' conviction that they are on the right side—indeed, that they are on the side which will ultimately triumph. Even Abbie Hoffman's playful style and satirical seriousness is supported by this hope. In reflecting on what might be worse than death, he muses: "I don't know. Surrendering. . . . Maybe nothing is really bad, since I am so convinced that we will win the future."[28] Hope has erupted as a constitutive element in some radical life styles. At a mass rally held at the Coliseum during the Democratic National Convention of 1968 Phil Ochs strummed and sang his ballads of protest and peace. Each time he came to the phrases "I Ain't Marching Anymore" and "The War Is Over," he was stopped by the ecstatic frenzy of the crowd who embraced, jumped, and cheered for several minutes before allowing him to continue. Facing the dangers which awaited them on the streets, the demonstrators were convinced that because the war should be over for the nation it should be over for them. Consequently, they would have no part of it. They weren't marching anymore. A young draft resister in our congregation expressed it this way in a letter to his local board:

> The war is over! No longer are we to fight the wars of the kingdoms of this world, which are fought with the weapons that kill men's bodies; instead we are called to fight the Lamb's War, which is fought with the weapons that heal men's souls. We are called to spread the word, for America today is like Andrew Jackson, who fought the Battle of New Orleans because he had not heard that the War of 1812 was over.[29]

The Leftist mood embodies many accents which are secular counterparts of the theology of hope. An often quoted aphorism is that of the Marxist, Ernst Bloch: "What is, cannot be true." I have heard New Left people express it in the following way: "When is this messed-up society going to quit using its TV tube to depict this fake world as it is and begin telling us about the real world that might be?" Herbert Marcuse affirms art as a means of protest to what is. In this vein he defines poetry as "the effort

79

which makes live in us that which does not exist."[30] It is evident that the New Left's desire to "imminentize the Eschaton," as charged by William F. Buckley, Jr., resembles the Christian hope which looks to the future for the reality of God but sees this reality as breaking into the present as a powerful force.

NOT RADICAL ENOUGH

New Leftists have often been criticized for wanting to overthrow the System but not offering anything better to take its place. Whereas the Old Left was attacked because of its doctrinaire ideology and its programmed revolutionary style, the New Left has been chastised for its failure to devise new patterns of social organization. Thus Christopher Lasch feels that "As long as the Left merely reacts to events, exposing and disrupting the 'system' without offering anything to take its place, it suffers endless defeats and frustrations out of which grow, not a consciousness of alternatives, but a rising demand for more and more militant tactics."[31] From a Christian perspective, I have been glad that the New Left repudiated the ideological dogmatism and utopian programs of the Old Left. In this they have often manifested a sense of openness to the future which is somewhat similar to the eschatological spirit of the New Testament. But I also believe that the New Left is not hopeful, not forward-looking enough. Without a vision of man as he should be, as defined in the picture of Jesus as the Christ, or a notion of the world as it should be, as pictured in the visions of the kingdom, the radical often becomes more of a specialist in what is wrong with the world than in what can be made right. Without radical enough hope in the coming of the kingdom, the Movement is vulnerable to moods of disillusionment, cynicism, and hopelessness.

This pessimism can lead to an attempt to implement the judgment which belongs to God alone. Such an effort has been expressed in tactics of disruption, in which a deliberate effort has been made to bring about repression from the System in order to victimize and radicalize increasing numbers of people. It is one thing to possess an apocalyptic faith which may expect things to get worse before they get better, with the realization that oppressive persecution may result from faithful witness. It is another thing, however, to deliberately strive to make things worse by seeking persecution, repression, and a denial of personal freedoms. Such neglects the Old Testament and Pauline interpretation of God: "Vengeance is mine, I will repay, says the Lord" (Rom. 12:19).

Such an effort at deliberate disruption results from a conception which points to the difference between religiously motivated revolution and the revolution of a secular ideology. R. W. Tucker defines the difference in this way: "Christians understand that the Kingdom comes as a gift from God, not at the end of a human struggle."[32] He quickly adds, however, that this does not mean a quietistic inactivity; the Christian must live now as though the kingdom were already realized, because for him it is. This contrast is also noted by Carl Braaten: "...the future in secular futurology is *reached* by a process of the world's *becoming.* The future in Christian eschatology *arrives* by the *coming* of God's kingdom."[33] Braaten nevertheless feels that there awaits a fruitful dialogue between theologians of Christian eschatology and proponents of secular futurology.

The New Left certainly offers one of the most fruitful areas of dialogue and cooperation for radical Christians. Since the New Left is very much in flux and spawns youth in search of new models of commitment, there exists a ready constituency for expressions of radical Christian faith. The Jesus freak movement is an example of this. Its danger may lie in a tendency to neglect the Kingdom motif of the Gospels in an exclusive preoccupation with a personal Jesus. The situation presents a bold challenge to Christians to put their faith into practice. Richard Shaull has observed that "The frontier for the theologian is not determined by an irrelevant orthodoxy and naive liberalism in the church, but by the defensiveness and blindness of representatives of a frightened establishment and the confusion and near despair in the ranks of the new revolutionaries."[34]

Prophetic Christian communities must seek out and support members of the youth culture, engaging them in reflection on the problems all radicals face and pointing to a hope which is too easy to relinquish in chaotic times. Alternatively, as recipients of the Christian tradition and language, these same communities should be able to interpret to unsympathetic middle-class Christians the meaning of the revolutionary movements of our time and their relationship to the faith of the apostles.

CHAPTER V

A Social Gospel for Today

Whatever their self-identity, those who espouse messianic, political, revolutionary, and radical themes in theology must recognize the legacy of the American Social Gospel Movement. As many young radicals define themselves in reference to the political liberalism they once believed but now repudiate, radical theologizing cannot escape its indebtedness to the themes and goals of the Social Gospel. During the heyday of neoorthodoxy, those who had not come to the new orthodoxy through theological liberalism were suspect. Since neoorthodoxy represented in so many ways a critique of liberalism, it was felt that someone who had not come this route might lack the perception and humility of a chastised liberal. Similarly, in the area of political and social action, neoorthodox converts who retained any social passion did so in the framework of revisions of the Social Gosepl. Allowing for the current input into theological radicalism from secular and evangelical circles, it is nevertheless true that most theological radicals have been cradled in one way or another in the matrix of the social and kingdom emphases of religious liberalism. For myself the identification of Christianity with social justice, racial equality, and world peace first came alive through an encounter with such concretions of the Social Gospel Movement in the thirties as cooperatives, work camps in slum areas, race relations laboratories, and international relations institutes.

"Social Christianity" had its origin in the "new theology" of the last decades of the nineteenth century. One of its chief proponents was Washington Gladden, who reached the acme of his influence as pastor of the First Congregational Church at Columbus, Ohio, from 1882 to the end of his life in 1918. Often honored as the father of the Social Gospel Movement, Gladden's early interest in the problems of labor coincided with his development of an ethicized and kingdom-centered theology. The "new theology" reached its peak and received its name in the first two decades of the twentieth century, primarily through the writings of Walter Rauschenbusch, whose last book was entitled *A Theology for the Social Gospel* (1917). These same themes were developed in various directions by an influential and brilliant cluster of scholars at the University of Chicago from 1906 to 1939. This "Chicago School of Theology" included such names as George Foster, Shirley Jackson Case, Gerald Birney Smith, Shailer Mathews, and Edward Scribner Ames.

Both at the beginning of the century and during its brief revival in the thirties, the great interest in social Christianity encompassed varying perspectives. On the left were those who imbibed Christian socialism, despaired completely of American and ecclesiastical institutions, and even defected altogether to Marxist and socialist circles. On the right there remained a brand of conservative social Christianity that expressed a concern for the poor (such as the Salvation Army) or a cause (such as the temperance societies) without disturbing the religious individualism which was the legacy of revivalism. In the middle there evolved a moderate or progressive social Christianity which became the dominant Social Gospel Movement and spawned the famous "Social Creed of the Churches" at the first meeting of the Federal Council of Churches in 1912. It was this group which came to control the denominational machinery of so-called liberal Protestantism in the decades following. This movement purported to remain rooted in the Christian tradition at the same time it attempted to be relevant to the new era of science, evolution, and industrialism.

Many would share Charles Hopkins' evaluation that the Social

Gospel has been "America's most unique contribution to the ongoing stream of Christianity."[1] Reacting to revivalist individualism, Social Gospel advocates sought to illustrate their convictions about the solidarity of the race with a concern for poverty, vice, crime, and labor strife in the cities. Though assuming a view of man and of progress which was later to be attacked as naive, the American gospel proceeded subtly to convert Europeans. A prime example is Dietrich Bonhoeffer, who came as a young Barthian to study at Union Theological Seminary in 1930-31. At the same time he attacked the lack of confessional standards and the theological illiteracy of the American students, he received from them another dimension in his desire to concretize the gospel. His visits to Harlem, his observation of the vigorous life in American churches, and his friendship with such men as Reinhold Niebuhr, Paul Lehmann, and Henry Sloane Coffin, returned Bonhoeffer to his teaching and to the slums of Berlin with a secular concern that was later to emerge as a major theological motif.

THE CONTEMPORANEITY OF THE SOCIAL GOSPEL

> *We have a social gospel. We need a systematic theology large enough to match it and vital enough to back it.*[2]

Walter Rauschenbusch's challenge has been echoed in our own day by Harvey Cox: "We are trying to live in a period of revolution without a theology of revolution. The development of such a theology should be the first item on the theological agenda today."[3] And Cox's own beginning in explicating secular themes as a foundation for a theology of social change immediately elicited comparisons with the Social Gospel. Papers were read at scholarly meetings and articles appeared in journals debating whether *The Secular City* was a revisiting of the Social Gospel.[4] It is, in fact, helpful to discern the contemporaneity of many themes of the older Social Gospel Movement.

Not surprisingly, as I have tried to indicate, Rauschenbusch found antecedents for his "new theology" in the roots of the

Christian faith and in the Reformation Radicals. The Social Gospel was not novel, but "a revival of the earliest doctrines of Christianity, of its radical ethical spirit, and of its revolutionary consciousness."[5] As a professor, Rauschenbusch pursued the research of his father, August Rauschenbusch, in the literature and outlook of the sixteenth-century sectarians, and his conscious identity with left-wing English and continental radicals is documented by his frequent references to them in his writings.[6]

Given the continuity of history, it is not surprising, then, to find in Gladden and Rauschenbusch, themes that reappear whenever a radical mood emerges anew. The contemporary conjoining of ethics, eschatology, and theology is but a continuation of the insistence of the Social Gospel that theology be moral and ethical. Doctrinal beliefs must be reflected in Christian living and action. Their affirmation of the secular resulted in extending the revivalist call beyond individuals to include all of society. The church's mission, according to Gladden, is not to save souls out of the world but to save the world. Moltmann quotes approvingly a similar view from Rauschenbusch: "Ascetic Christianity called the world evil and left it. Humanity is waiting for a revolutionary Christianity which will call the world evil and change it."[7]

The most fundamental continuity between current radical theologizing and the Social Gospel is in the common appropriation of the biblical motif of the kingdom as the central theme. Rauschenbusch viewed the kingdom ideal as containing the revolutionary force of Christianity and attempted to systematize all other doctrines around it. Similar to current usage, he defined the kingdom of God as "history seen in a religious and teleological way," as "humanity organized according to the will of God," and as "the power of the coming age."[8] In the literature of the Social Gospel the marks of the kingdom are given as love, justice, freedom, service, growth, solidarity, and the worth of each human personality.

The idea of solidarity provides a clue to understanding such traditional doctrines as original sin and atonement. Instead of rejecting the notion of sin as is often charged, proponents of the

Social Gospel reinterpreted sin in terms of a solidaristic and organic conception of the power and reality of evil in the world. Original sin refers more to the universality of sin and our mutual interdependence than to any biological inheritance. An updated manifestation of this view would be the explosion of an atomic weapon made possible through the collective effort and money of millions and in turn bringing evil to millions. Thus, Rauschenbusch can speak of nations and communities of men as becoming super-personal forces of evil, or the kingdom of evil. He maintained that "The higher the institution, the worse it is when it goes wrong."[9] This view of sin leads to a major premise of the Social Gospel, one with a contemporary ring, namely, that judgment must be proclaimed against collective institutions.

It was natural that Rauschenbusch preferred the ethical and social definition of sin as selfishness, which definition he regarded as Hebraic, to the more dualistic conception of the Greek Fathers, who thought of sin as sensuousness and materiality. Sin, according to Rauschenbusch, is not so much a violation of ceremonial or religious codes as the lack of proper relationship between men. The realization of sin comes in the contrast of our lives and the nature of our society with the ideals of social righteousness contained in the person of Christ and the kingdom of God.

This focus on the kingdom motif may have contributed to the anti-ecclesiastical bias of both the Social Gospel and contemporary radical Christianity. Rauschenbusch felt that when the kingdom ceased to be a dominant reality in Christian consciousness, the church moved in to take its place as the object of supreme good. The church was not intended to be identified with the kingdom; it was but a means to bring in the kingdom. The current language about the church's being a proleptic or provisional sign to anticipate that which God intends for all humanity is very similar to the Social Gospel hope that ultimately the lines between church and world would disappear. Likewise Rauschenbusch's reasoning that great criticisms of the church are in reality a form of compliment since they discern the potential nature and capacity of the church, should be heard as a comforting note by weary ecclesiastics. His view of baptism as a revolutionary act of allegiance to a new order of things rather than an act to save self, and his association of the Lord's Supper with the realization of the mission of the church jibe with our previous analyses of these doctrines in the context of the Radical Reformation.[10]

Though not entirely relinquishing the notion of transcendence, the Social Gospel strongly emphasized God's immanence. This theme of the fatherhood of God finds its modern counterpart in the frequent references to the activity of God in history. Though the predominant humanism may have been inadequate at certain points, the stress on the goodness and worth of man is akin to the current themes of new humanity, new optimism, and man's responsibility. Though many of us would not enthusiastically follow Edward Ames in preaching on Lincoln eleven times in one year and ceremoniously receiving him into the fellowship of our local congregation, the great emphasis on democracy still finds echoes in the New Left slogan of participatory democracy and in new manifestations of the lay apostolate in Christendom. We shall note later some basic discontinuities in messianic and apocalyptic exegesis. Here, Rauschenbusch should be hailed as a forerunner to all theologians of hope in his assertion that "Religion is always eschatological. Its characteristic is faith. It lives in and for the future."[11] The contemporaneity of many of the accents of the Social Gospel can be further seen in the renewed interest in "The Chicago School of Theology," the appropriation by Old Testament scholars of the Social Gospel's sense of solidarity, and the attention paid to Walter Rauschenbusch by such current scholars as Moltmann.

THE ACHILLES HEEL OF THE SOCIAL GOSPEL

> A God without wrath brought men without sin into a kingdom without judgment through the ministrations of a Christ without a cross.[12]

This famous—and unfair—caricature of the Social Gospel by H.

Richard Niebuhr represents the mood of a generation reacting against the naive optimism and humanism of their progenitors. For in the Social Gospel Movement the advent of the kingdom came to be identified all too often with the secular doctrine of progress. This doctrine had its origin in the Enlightenment's faith in the possibilities of man's upward movement through history and found scientific confirmation in Darwin's theories of evolution. A secularized version of the doctrine of providence, this faith in progress viewed history as having moved and as continuing to move in a desirable direction. The ape and the tiger in the bosom of man was about to die. Overcoming the cultural gap would mean that having come out of the jungle scientifically, man would now come out morally and spiritually. "If the external signs could be trusted," Gladden wrote, "there would be good reason for believing that the day is not far distant when it [Christianity] will take full possession of the earth."[13] A young Disciple editor named his paper *The Christian Century* in the exuberant spirit of an age which felt that the long-awaited millennium without war or poverty might be imminent. And Rauschenbusch closes his last book with the feeling that in the new century "The era of prophetic and democratic Christianity has just begun."[14]

A developmental view of the kingdom came to be articulated in opposition to the strong currents of premillennialism of the time. Gladden objected to the millennial expectations because they focused on an otherworldly future rather than on the present, sought to save the individual from the world instead of redeeming the world, and were characterized by a pessimism about society which paralyzed efforts for change.[15] Rauschenbusch did not reject the millennial idea; rather, he sought to reinterpret it. "Church historians," he wrote, "usually dwell on the theological objections to the carnal millennial ideas, but fail to see how distasteful the social elements of the millennial ideal must have been to those who controlled the teaching of the Church."[16] He agreed with the this-worldly aspects of the millennial hope, but felt that the emphasis must be shifted from

89

catastrophic to developmental interpretations, as Jesus provided in his parables of growth. It was in these parables, said Rauschenbusch, that Jesus emancipated himself from the prevailing apocalyptic world view.

In spite of the tendencies of some of their followers, the fathers of social Christianity did not propose an easy, automatic ushering in of the kingdom. Though he believed progress to be certain, Gladden felt it would be irregular. Following a Hegelian scheme, he advocated a law of progress through successive antagonisms. Rauschenbusch, likewise, did not envisage the arrival of the kingdom without intense struggle with the kingdom of evil. Neither did he assume the utopianism which often accompanies teleological philosophies of history: "An eschatology which is expressed in terms of historical development has no final consummation. Its consummations are always the basis for further development. The Kingdom of God is always coming, but we can never say 'Lo here'."[17]

In spite of these emendations, adding ingredients of opposition and conflict, the basic liberal-bourgeois trust in natural harmony remained, along with its assumption that our society was moving progressively toward greater good for all in a basically orderly way. It was believed that such change could occur within the framework of institutional continuity without upsetting our values and lives. But this optimism was, of course, doomed to eventual disillusionment—for the same reason the schemes of the chiliastic prophets came to be rejected. The promises of the coming kingdom were simply not realized in the chaos and horror of the twentieth century.

Today, the prevalent rejection of the doctrine of progress indicates our entirely different situation. Proponents of a Social Gospel at the beginning of our century viewed as the chief obstructionists to social change those who so despaired of progress that they adopted a literalized, futurized, and schematized apocalypticism. This mood seemed to say: "The world is getting worse! Hallelujah! This means we are nearer the time when Jesus will come and make all things right as is predicted." Today the enemy is more likely to be the gradualist than the premillennialist. Many contemporary advocates for radical change oppose those evolutionists who are so convinced that things will work out that they try to prevent change and who compromise with evil in order not to upset an ordered society.

Men today are becoming aware that our time is growing increasingly apocalyptic. The premillennial and chiliastic preachers, though they fell into the pitfalls of literalization, turned out to be discerning prophets in sensing that all was not going well in an era confident that science would usher in the golden age. Today, the scientists themselves have become apocalyptists, warning of possible annihilation unless there are radical changes in the environment and in population control. The very technological revolution which was hailed as the savior of mankind is now feared as the archenemy.

A natural corollary to the doctrine of progress was a rather high assessment of man. Though Rauschenbusch's theology was more realistic than Gladden's assertions about the natural goodness of man, a major portion of the Social Gospel Movement came to believe in man's basic rationality and good will. Through education men could be led to prefer social good over private advantage. Science was an ally and not an enemy of the faith, providing the methodology whereby the great revolution already effected in the physical world could be duplicated in the social order. Most advocates of the Social Gospel presupposed an epistemology which found religious authority in man's intuition and experience, his reason and moral sensitivity. This overconfidence in basic rationality led to the existentialist reaction, and the one-sided stress on basic goodness set the stage for the neoorthodox critiques, one of the most brilliant that of Reinhold Niebuhr.

In one sense this movement did not completely escape the individualism of the revivalist atmosphere which nurtured it. Rather than opting for socialism, Gladden chose as his model a socialized individual transformed by the love commandment. One gets the impression that the Social Gospel theologians were struggling to bring together two definitions of salvation which they regarded to be quite distinct and separate. Regenerate individuals were essential, they asserted, in order to work for the redemption of society. The personal gospel and the social gospel both have a place in this framework. Many contemporary radicals, on the contrary, view the personal and social dimensions of salvation as integrally related in biblical definitions. Whereas for the earlier prophets of social Christianity, the personal and social were bipolar aspects of the gospel, today they appear to be more dialectical.

THE RELEVANCE OF THE EARLY REINHOLD NIEBUHR

The rediscovery of the Marxism and radicalism of the early Reinhold Niebuhr may not only be relevant to the growing dialogue between Christians and Marxists but may also help to clarify the issues involved in any radical critique of the Social Gospel. Along with that of Walter Rauschenbusch and Martin Luther King, Reinhold Niebuhr's contribution to Christian ethics will, no doubt, prove to be among the most significant in the twentieth century. Like Rauschenbusch and King, he was a parish preacher who was propelled to prominence through his pastoral involvement in the political and economic struggles of his parishioners. Finding himself preaching to workers battling with the new automobile industry in Detroit from 1915 to 1928, Niebuhr departed from his liberal orientation in coming to feel that force and collective coercion, in addition to moral persuasion and education, were required if justice was to win the day.

Niebuhr's subsequent professorship at Union Theological Seminary and his brilliant theological articulation of realistic and neoorthodox views of man are well known. In his pilgrimage he moved from a position of radical judgment on society to a more pragmatic social analysis. From a revolutionary stance with Marxist overtones, he moderated into the mainstream of liberalism, becoming one of the founders of Americans for Democratic Action. From a suspect leftist, Niebuhr came to be one of the most respected theoreticians for those political scientists in the forties and fifties who were seeking theological props for the great war against fascism, the cold war against Communism, and an apologetic for realpolitik. Now, in light of the fact that many prophetic Christians have moved or been thrust from mainstream political activity, the radical critiques of the young pastor and professor may offer a more pertinent critique of the Social Gospel than his later position. Some of the articles written by Niebuhr for *The World Tomorrow* from 1928 to 1933 are especially exciting. That this periodical represented well the ideology of the Social Gospel is revealed by the subtitle on one of the editorial pages: "A Journal Looking Toward a Social Order Based on the Religion of Jesus." Its theological liberalism is also attested by the men who served as Niebuhr's coeditors and contributing editors, such men as Kirby Page, John Nevin Sayre, Paul H. Douglas, Sherwood Eddy, John Haynes Homes, Rufus M. Jones, A. J. Muste, and Norman Thomas. Though Niebuhr was willing to identify with the Social Gospel Movement and these men, his early writings reveal basic differences as well as a restlessness with the movement.

In an article entitled "Is Peace or Justice the Goal?" in the September 21, 1932, issue of *The World Tomorrow,* Niebuhr deals with the relation of the doctrine of man to Christian radicalism.[18] He first applauds the champions of radicalism from the earliest times to the present. While it is true that the great bulk of the religious community usually sides with political and social conservatism, says Niebuhr, the presence of radicalism refutes the charge that Christianity is necessarily an opiate to the people. But unfortunately, he continues, radicals too often have little understanding of man's weakness: "Our own modern radical Christianity has been far too intimately associated with conventional religious liberalism to have a realistic estimate of human nature."[19] Calling Rauschenbusch "the founder of American Christian radicalism" and praising his zeal for an ideal that was essentially socialistic, Niebuhr nevertheless felt that Rauschenbusch did not grasp the necessity of class conflict. Instead, Rauschenbusch expected, as so many educators and sociologists did, that a just society can be built through education and moral persuasion. Niebuhr, in his later *Moral Man and Immoral Society*, was extremely critical of the optimism of modern educators. Whereas religion expected to bring about an ideal society by the conversion of individuals, it was now proposed, Niebuhr observed, to do it by educating them. "If anything," he argued, "the modern educator is even more romantic than the modern liberal Christian. The Christian has something in his tradition about all men being sinners. . . ."[20] Because of this naiveté about human nature, Niebuhr charged, the privileged classes can enjoy the luxury of believing that necessary change will come through the growing unselfishness of man, which is then documented by every charitable gesture of the men of power and privilege. But Christian radicalism, which is just beginning to free itself from the dogmas of Christian liberalism, must accept the idea of class struggle. In Niebuhr's early writings this anthropological realism did not lead as much to pointing out the moral ambiguities of ethical decisions as it did in his later work. Instead, his realism was in the context of asserting that society needed more the challenge of the absolutists than the sweet reasonableness of the rationalists.[21] He did advocate that the radical try to confine his opposition in the struggle to nonviolent means.

The problem of the use of violence in the class struggle raises the question of pacifism. Niebuhr, who for several years was national chairman of the Fellowship of Reconciliation, broke definitely with the pacifist position in 1932 and was destined to become one of the most brilliant critics of liberal pacifism. However, his own position in the years immediately preceding 1932 was not at all typical of the dominant theology of the postwar peace movement. This can be detected in the article "Pacifism and the Use of Force," which appeared in *The World Tomorrow* in 1928.[22] Niebuhr's brand of pacifism here raises the question of whether he might have been driven out of the peace movement by its lack of biblical realism and political radicalism as much as by any fundamental changes in his own thinking. In this article Niebuhr refuses to accept the pacifism of the left which repudiates the use of force in all situations. Instead, he identifies with a pacifism of the right which holds that the use of physical violence in international life is an unjustified evil but that some force may be necessary in specific situations.[23]

"Pacifists assume too easily," Niebuhr wrote, "that all controversies are due to misunderstandings which might be solved by a greater degree of imagination."[24] In reality the strong are not convinced to stop their exploitation until the weak offer resistance. Oppressed peoples are forced to appeal to more than the imagination and innate sense of justice of their oppressors. Yet it is possible to resist injustice without using physical force and resorting to violence, for one may inflict damage on the oppressor through such devices as economic boycotts and strikes. Niebuhr's analysis of the possible results of violence is interesting in light of our own situation:

> When oppressed groups resort to violence, they also confuse the moral judgment of the society from which they seek justice. They give the society the pretext for identifying social maladjustments with social peace and for maintaining the former in the effort to preserve the latter. In the same way the effort of society to maintain a social equilibrium by the undue use of force, particularly by the violent use of force, inevitably confuses rather than clarifies the moral judgments of its minorities and easily prompts them to violence and destruction.[25]

In this Niebuhr would doubtless have agreed with the oft-quoted statement of John F. Kennedy that those who make peaceful revolutions impossible make violent revolutions inevitable. Niebuhr introduces into the discussion the analogy of the criminal. Although some force may be necessary in dealing with the criminal, it is urgent that one use as little as possible. Likewise, "every undue reliance upon force obscures the defects in the life of society itself which have helped to create the criminal."[26]

Niebuhr's summary statement, which affirms pacifism in spite of its pitfalls, is especially interesting in the light of the many subsequent debates:

> The validity of the pacifist position rests in a general way upon the assumption that men are intelligent and moral and that a generous attitude toward them will ultimately, if not always immediately discover, develop and challenge what is best in them. This is a large assumption which every specific instance will not justify. The strategy of love therefore involves some risks. These risks are not as great as they are sometimes made to appear, for the simple reason that love does not only discover but it creates moral purpose.[27]

Niebuhr was already beginning to point to man's limitedness and his collective egoism over against those who stress man's limitless capacity for transformation. But as he failed to do later, Niebuhr was also affirming the transforming power of love against those who lay a one-sided stress on man's sinfulness. Even though he was to depart even further from this chastened pacifism, he continued for many years to favor nonviolent over violent resistance whenever possible. He always insisted, however, that the pacifist recognize that nonviolence is seldom free from a type of force and from moral ambiguity.

Niebuhr's recognition of the nature of class conflict and the necessity of organized resistance to exploitation reveals his early Marxist orientation. We can see the present relevance of his attempt to organically relate the Social Gospel to Marxist radicalism when we note that while we may be living in a post-Christian era, we are not in a post-Marxist one. Among students and minorities and for increasing numbers in the third world, Marxism-Leninism is still the bearer of the revolutionary spirit in our time. In his essay "Marxism and Religion," in *The World Tomorrow* (March, 1933), we find an excellent statement of Niebuhr's pertinence to the current dialogue between Christianity and Marxism.[28] This article deals primarily with those elements in middle-class Protestantism which make them a counterrevolutionary rather than a revolutionary force in society. Niebuhr feels that the radical Marxist critique is not mistaken in its evaluation of Protestantism as a whole, but that it is often wrong in its failure to apply the same critique to other institutions of middle-class life. The university in Niebuhr's time was especially lacking in radical outlook. Far more clergymen than university professors, Niebuhr claimed, were in intimate contact with the poor. The basic mistake of the secular or Marxist radical, therefore, has been to regard religion per se, instead of the religion of the entrenched social classes as inimical to the proletarian cause. It has been the individualistic philosophy of the middle classes that has espoused an otherworldliness which thinks of redemption only in personal rather than social terms and which forces this gospel on the more ignorant and passive poor as an opiate.

Another aspect of religious otherworldliness promulgated by the ruling classes consists in finding "the basis of happiness in inner values which transcend external and social circumstances. . . .The ability to reconcile men to the inevitable and to give them inner security against the most untoward circumstances. . .can easily be used by a dominant group to persuade a subject class into acquiescence."[29] Niebuhr is caustic in his criticism of the vulgarity and hypocrisy of the owning classes, who give the impression that they are indifferent to material things only after they have taken care of their most extravagant material wishes. Yet another aspect of middle-class religion which makes it an opiate for the people is the doctrine of progress to which I have referred, a doctrine which does not deal with the realities of social conflict. Here the religious Establishment attempts to persuade those suffering from injustice to patiently wait until their oppressors have learned how to be decent and unselfish. Niebuhr rightly points out the hypocrisy of this moral perfectionism which allows a dominant class to profit by the use of power and violence while counseling the dispossessed not to resort to force in order to gain freedom. "The Christian idea of love is rightly discounted today because it is used to stabilize a world reeking with injustice."[30]

In contrast to the religion used as an opiate by the Establishment, the religion of the more virile elements among the disinherited, Niebuhr asserts, "has always expressed itself in apocalyptic visions of a redeemed society."[31] This is in line with the more Hebraic idea of salvation found in the prophets and in Jesus, which is this-worldly. Niebuhr believes that it is possible "to develop a rebellious energy against every form of social injustice and yet maintain the religious assurance that 'life consisteth not in the abundance of things a man possesseth.' " He feels that this is just as possible as for a man to seek the elimination of his disease and yet recognize that he will not be happy simply in possessing physical health. "A religious idealism which is organically related to Marxian radicalism will first of all fight for bread and security for everyone. Only by doing that will it be in a position to maintain that man does not live by bread alone."[32]

Walter Rauschenbusch had gone a long way in his critique of capitalism. "If we can trust the Bible," he wrote, "God is against capitalism, its methods, spirit, and results. The bourgeois theologians have misrepresented our revolutionary God."[33] We have seen that Niebuhr went beyond even this and attempted to integrally relate secular and Christian radicalism. Though he later repudiated much of his early Marxist orientation, his radical liberalism anticipated much that has been happening three decades later. Niebuhr's first chastised version of the Social Gospel has much to offer for reformulations of that gospel today.

THE RADICALIZATION OF LIBERALISM

Because of its liberal rhetoric, some maintain that the Port Huron statement of the Students for Democratic Society (1962) could never have been the foundation for a new radicalism. Others argue that it is precisely this liberal base which has been the springboard for the radicalization of so many. The brief biographies of young radicals frequently tell of youths who had been campaigning for liberal candidates and values and were radicalized in attempting to live out their liberal assumptions. Similarly, it has been a deep frustration with mainline political liberalism that has radicalized many churchmen. A delineation of the shifts involved in the radicalization of the liberal Christian may help us in our effort to define a Social Gospel for our day.

Consistent with its doctrine of progress and its high estimate of human nature, the old Social Gospel thought it could save the social order by Christianizing it. The statements of contemporary radical ethicists are much less confident. The sentiment of Max L. Stackhouse is typical: "We do not claim to *have* a message of redemption and sanctification that needs only to be implemented in the social order to be fulfilled."[34] Rather than build the kingdom, many feel that the proper response is to proclaim its coming and to participate in it. "God's kingdom is still coming," writes Frederick Herzog, but "we are not called upon to bring it in. We are only asked to witness to the reign of Christ, already begun, by changing society in ways that open up the future."[35] The shift from the older to the newer social Christianity is a shift from pragmatic strategy to radical witness. Current radical moods stress not so much the construction of a revolution from man's own resources as a response to God's grace which is historically mediated. Rather than updating Christianity to make it more relevant to the needs of the times, radical Christianity tries to recover the revolutionary and eschatological message of primitive Christianity. Lacking strong bases for optimism in the activity of man, the radical faith bases its optimism on a more theocentric and christocentric faith. Such faith, however, does not imply a mood of resignation which leaves everything to God. Rather it sees the breaking in of God's future as an explosive and liberating power which elicits a revolutionary response from man.

It is worth noting the difference in the center of activity for the old and new Social Gospels. The centers of action for the older Social Gospel Movement was the church, since the most exciting proclamations came from the pulpit. The older movement was primarily a preaching movement, as Robert Handy points out:

> Though the social gospel did call for action and did encourage responsible participation in philanthropic and political causes for the righting of social wrongs, its leaders were not so much activists as they were preachers, proclaimers, and educators. They sought to

change men's views and attitudes, to win them to a new religio-social faith.[36]

Washington Gladden had maintained that it was the pastor and not the church who was free to advocate such schemes as industrial cooperatives, profit-sharing, and union organization. The job of the church was to inspire individuals, who in turn would implement these manifestations of brotherhood in economic life. Thus, the old Social Gospel advocates were educators; the new Social Gospel attracts activists. The place of action has moved from the pulpit to the streets. Reporters used to gather news for their religious pages and columns by learning what was to be said in the key pulpits of any major city; today, the situation is much more complicated. Religious news reporters find themselves investigating not so much the pulpit but the activity, involvements, conflicts, special ministries, and programs of avant-garde clergy and laymen.

Because action poses a more genuine threat to the status quo than pulpit rhetoric, a social Christianity for our day may be surrounded with much more controversy than before. The opposition will not be limited to conservative members who maintain that the church has no business in politics; unlike its predecessors, the current movement will experience bitter opposition from the powers-that-be in local and national life. As men like Washington Gladden and Edward Ames irenically sought to avoid conflict and often preferred peace to justice, current Christian radicals feel that as a prelude to reconciliation they must prophetically bring to the surface the deep alienations resulting from injustice.

Current preachers can still get into trouble in many pulpits by denying the literal historicity of the Genesis narratives; however, they may arouse still more ire by defending black power or making a basic judgment against American foreign policy. Whereas young seminarians used to get into the most trouble with conservative congregations, on suspicion of heresy, many young Christian radicals today are likely to provoke the greatest opposition from liberal congregations weighted with members of the local Establishment. And such opposition is more determined because prophetic action poses more of a threat to the church's respectability than does prophetic preaching alone.

In reporting on a 1969 Resistance Conference, Staughton Lynd shared in a speech an observation that in many ways summarizes the basic shift we have been discerning from a more liberal to a radical stance:

> Liberalism, Greg Calvert asserted, is based on the psychology of guilt and on the program of helping others to achieve what one already has. On the other hand, radicalism stems from "the perception of oneself as unfree, as oppressed" and expresses itself in "a struggle for collective liberation of all unfree, oppressed men."[37]

Whereas the liberal Social Gospel preachers appealed to their people to help *others,* the laboring classes and the poor in their struggles for justice, contemporary radical expressions assert that we all share in the depersonalization, the false priorities, the racism, and the sins of militarism of modern society. Liberalism knew a politics based on guilt; radicalism is espousing a politics of liberation. From a paternalistic concern about those who are underprivileged, we have come to see that our present situation is one that oppresses us all.

Because of its epistemological idealism, the Social Gospel Movement stressed the need for a conversion of the mind. But the subsequent rediscovery of biblical realism about man and the pressure of times which are definitely apocalyptic have called forth a Social Gospel that demands a conversion of life style. The strategies that come from a radical stance—which have been only partially defined here—will be the subject of the last chapter. In the next chapter I want to examine the revolutionary, messianic, and apocalyptic motifs of the biblical message itself.

CHAPTER VI

The Revolutionary Apocalypse

Radical Christians are enthusiastically appropriating the revolutionary, messianic, and apocalyptic motifs of the Bible. This may represent little more than an exercise in proof texting, in which we attempt to buttress our own biases and program through an appeal to respected authority. On the other hand, the reappearance of these themes may be God's way of enlivening and empowering his Word for our day. The setting and meaning of these biblical motifs have been the object of extensive exegesis by many current scholars. This chapter will present only an inadequate summary of some of their conclusions. I hope, however, that it will succeed in illuminating our basic thesis defining radical as both revelational and revolutionary.

REVOLUTIONARY ROOTS

If revolution implies change affecting every aspect of life, the message of the early Christians was revolutionary. "Here was a *revolutionary* God, releasing *revolutionary power* through a *revolutionary community*, in *revolutionary action.*"[1] Such theological affirmations about the nature of the primitive faith must not be made in isolation from the milieu of the early movement. Politically, Christianity was cradled in a revolutionary context. In the year 160 B.C., Judas the Maccabee and his brothers had ushered in a century of Jewish freedom through zealous, bloody, and fierce guerrilla warfare. Maintained by many violent scrimmages, this respite from foreign domination lasted until 63 B.C., when the Roman general Pompey desecrated the temple, slaughtering the officiating priests and 12,000 Jews. In New Testament times, Palestine was occupied territory with the professional troops of Rome quartered on the countryside by a puppet administration. Growing up in the midst of the Galilean insurgency, Jesus may well have observed as a boy the suppression of an uprising in a nearby village. He was identified with a people who suffered under heavy taxation and despised the heavy yoke of Roman rule. This passionate spirit of Jewish nationalism led to the large-scale revolt of A.D. 66, which was climactically suppressed in the destruction of the temple in A.D. 70.

It was such a country, seething with years of revolutionary ferment and violence, that Christians have declared to be the spot where God sent his Son. In this milieu assertions that the kingdom was near carried revolutionary overtones. For example, teachings about going the second mile alluded to the unpopular demands of Roman soldiers to carry bags. Biblical scholars are currently debating the relationship of Jesus to the revolutionary Zealots. Was Jesus himself a revolutionary? If so, what kind? In considering the answers to these questions, it might be helpful to briefly examine the types of responses which surfaced in this revolutionary climate. The Sadducees, the Pharisees, the Essenes, and the Zealots were born in the midst of the Jewish freedom struggle during the generations immediately preceding the birth of Jesus.

THE SADDUCEES

Though the name "Sadducees" can be traced to Solomon's priest Zadok, the party emerged around 135-104 B.C., following the reorganization of Judaism undertaken by Maccabean leadership in order to gather a new high-priestly line out of the chaos and the discontinuities created by the revolutionary situation. We know them primarily through the writings of their detractors, and some of the common pejorative judgments may be lacking in firm historical support. Simply because we know of instances in which they were subversive, it is not fair to label them as total collaborators with the Romans. It is safe to assume, however, that the Sadducees became determined defenders of their priestly prerogatives as the new state evolved. And some did effectively exchange cooperation with their conquerors for the maintenance of their own priestly functions and interests. They regarded themselves as the primary interpreters of the law and were not as open to the oral law or to such new theological ideas as the doctrine of the resurrection as were their chief antagonists, the Pharisees. In contemporary parlance, the Sadducees were the religious conservatives of their day. Their counterparts are all of us who acquiesce and compromise with the injustices of the status quo to protect our own privileged positions. The New Testament writers picture Jesus as a friend of the poor, the outcasts, and the rebellious, and not as a man possessing close affinities with this party.

THE PHARISEES

The religious party referred to most often by the synoptic writers originated in the same period as the Sadducees, during the reign of the Hasmonean ruler John Hyrcanus (135-106 B.C.). They came to constitute a very influential force within Judaism, numbering some 6,000 men at the time of Jesus. They were popular religious teachers in the tradition of the lay scribes and early prophets. And like their early precursors, they found themselves pitted against the priestly and ruling classes.

In spite of—or because of—the many biblical references to them, the Pharisees remain something of an enigma. Since they were sticklers for the ritualism and legalism of their own tradition, they have commonly been regarded as religious conservatives. But on the other hand because their oral tradition remained in many ways flexible and adjustable, open to new ideas, they must be seen as the religious rationalists, progressives, and liberals of their day. Their modernism consisted in their receptivity to such new doctrinal emphases as the resurrection of the body, the idea of providence, and the coming of a messiah who would establish his kingdom. They were seeking a spiritual reformation within Judaism as the means to gain freedom from the Roman oppressors. In the pericopes narrating the popularity of Jesus as a teacher and in his designation as a Rabbi and prophet, Jesus is pictured as one who might well have been a Pharisee in the eyes of the people. And it has often been asserted that his severe and frequent criticism of this party may have resulted simply from his geographical and ideological proximity to them.

THE ESSENES

Sharing common roots with the Pharisees, the Essenes, too, became increasingly critical of the compromising stance of the other parties born during the revolutionary period. We have come to know more about this party through the discovery of the Dead Sea scrolls. It is estimated that they numbered some 4,000 in the New Testament era. The Essenes came to embody the strategy of a radical monastic community. They were scrupulous in avoiding ceremonial uncleanness. They lived simply, were communitarian in their view of property, practiced celibacy, and formulated rigid standards of admission and discipline. They looked forward to the day when the holy temple would be liberated from the degenerate priests, and their nation from Rome. Although some of the Essenes did participate later in armed insurrections, they were for the most part the purists, the communitarians, of their day. In contemporary language they represented those who were "cop-outs," those who were determined to "do their own thing" in trying times. John the Baptist was an Essene, and Jesus may have appeared a follower of him. But Jesus' mission was in fact a call to radical discipleship in the political arena and not a call to escape from it.

THE ZEALOTS

A fourth party to emerge during this period was truly revolutionary in the sense of violent. The Zealots stemmed from a movement led by Judas the Galilean in A.D. 6 for the purpose of resisting Roman rule. Many of the names of the Zealots—the Simons, the Judases, and the Johns—betray their identification with the early Maccabean freedom fighters. They attracted the militant and radical rebels against foreign domination. They also shared a zeal for the law of the Jews. Their hope was the hope of Israel for the restoration of independence. The Zealots were the patriots, the Jewish nationalists, the violent revolutionaries. They represented a vanguard cadre of the people in their hostility to the rich and sympathy for the poor. Their modern counterparts encompass the multitudes described by Franz Fanon, *The Wretched of the Earth*, who prefer the human dignity which accompanies violent resistance, even to death, to a living death under oppression.

It is the relationship of Jesus and his disciples to the Zealots that is providing one of the most intriguing discussions in contemporary New Testament studies. At the center of the debate is S. G. F. Brandon's scholarly work *Jesus and the Zealots*.[2] Unlike some, Brandon does not maintain that Jesus himself was strictly a Zealot. Rather, he argues that Jesus sympathized with the goals of the Zealots and advocated reforms which would aid their cause. After his death, the disciples and especially the Jewish Christian community at Jerusalem joined in the expectations that Jesus would be the Messiah who would come to crush the Romans and restore the kingdom of Israel. Since these Zealot and Jewish-Christian hopes were dashed in the destruction of the temple in A.D. 70, it was necessary to subsequently reinterpret the gospel to make it palatable to Greek culture and Roman rule. This process was begun by Stephen and Paul and completed by the Evangelists. They introduced pacifist, universalist, hellenistic, and individualistic elements into the kerygma of the church in order to clothe the original revolutionary messianic community with the accouterments of a mystery cult.

Brandon's own long tenure in the Chaplains Corps of the British Royal Army and his admiration for guerrilla warfare against imperialist powers may make him vulnerable to the peril of modernizing Jesus. Nevertheless, his work is being greeted as the first since Schweitzer's study to take seriously Jesus' own eschatological perspective. Others are also recognizing the close affinities with the Zealot movement. Some have conjectured that as many as half of the twelve disciples might have come from among these violent revolutionaries. We do definitely know that one was a Zealot; moreover, two were "sons of thunder" and others carried the names of popular Maccabean freedom fighters. Hans Werner Bartsch, a German New Testament scholar, believes similarly that Jesus sympathized with the Zealots and identified with them not only in his choosing of the twelve but in his fundamental attitudes. When Jesus said he would be counted among the outlaws, those outside of the law, he was according to Professor Bartsch identifying with the Zealots. Jesus was most likely put to death because Pilate, in agreement with the senate, was convinced that Jesus and his disciples were a part of the Zealot movement. The title "King of the Jews" which was written on the cross testifies to the economic and political threat Jesus posed to the Romans. In terms of sympathies, Jesus' frequent association with the poor, the prisoners, the dispossessed, the harlots, and sinners points to a basic identification with a first-century anti-establishment mood. It was the Son of Man who had no place to lay his head who became the paradigm for the Christian bias against the rich and its affirmation of the blessedness of the poor.

But while it recognizes many valid elements in Brandon's picture of Jesus, the strong consensus of scholarship still affirms fundamental discontinuities between Jesus and the Zealots. Although Jesus was not averse to being counted among the Zealots, says Professor Bartsch, he does not call upon his disciples to draw the sword. For the revolution was not to be ushered in by man but by God. There are many precedents in Jewish thought from which Jesus could have derived this perspective. Likewise, Brandon's thesis does not allow for the possibility that the canonical writings are accurate in reporting that Jesus' espousal of the way of the cross was a real scandal and the cause of much misunderstanding by his earliest followers. Many feel that in proposing a decisive discontinuity between the Christian movement and its origins Brandon's analysis cannot adequately account for the vitality of Christianity in the early centuries. Brandon and some modern analysts too quickly delimit the interpretive choices to two: collaboration or armed resistance, Hellenization or militant apocalypticism. What inaugurated the Christian movement may have been a new style of resistance. Thus, the judgment of the Romans that Jesus was a violent revolutionary may have been mistaken, just as the Establishment today fails to differentiate between violent and nonviolent revolutionaries. But even less accurate than the Zealot thesis have been those interpretations of many modern Christians that have made Jesus a counterrevolutionary unworthy of crucifixion. As Walter Wink observes:

> ...Brandon must be credited with at least revising the current image toward a deeper appreciation of the political context in which the protagonists and antagonists moved. Where he has not to my mind shown cause to believe that Jesus or the early Jewish Christians were favorably disposed toward the Zealot program or that they countenanced armed rebellion against Rome, he has succeeded in dispelling some of the pious aura which has obscured the lengths to which Jesus was willing to go to establish righteousness.[3]

Like the Sadducees, Jesus, in his revolutionary context, was for religion, but his religious zeal was directed to save others instead of himself. Like the Pharisees, he was interested in preserving the best in Judaism, but he insisted that love for people was more important than principles and that such love should be put into practice. Like the Essenes, he was for religious purity, but he refused the ritual purity of noninvolvement. He wanted to live out this purity in the world. He was most sympathetic to the cause of the Zealots, but he believed that evil would not ultimately be overcome with evil, but only with good. He rejected quietism (the Essenes), an alliance with the Establishment (the Sadducees), hypocritical popular religion (the Pharisees), and the idea of the crusade (the Zealots).

In terms of a fundamental departure from the *Zeitgeist* of his day, the nonviolent cross can be seen to ultimately constitute a more revolutionary way than that of the Zealots. Jesus may well have affirmed the Zealot passion for justice and the coming kingdom of righteousness while opposing their nationalistic fervor and revengeful spirit. His way of dying was a scandal to many because he chose the way of suffering love in the face of evil. However, this same cross remains a scandal to many contemporary disciples since he was crucified because he was indeed a type of revolutionary. Even if Jesus cannot be labeled a pure Zealot, the revolutionary "communist" of his day, he was not reluctant to associate or be identified with them, even to the extent of including them in his intimate circle. This realization has contributed to the current radicalization of theology.

MESSIANIC MESSAGE

The revolutionary situation of early Christianity served as the matrix for a revolutionary message. The current rediscovery of messianic, political, and apocalyptic themes in many of the canonical writers weakens Brandon's presupposition of the basic discontinuity between the activity of Jesus and the interpretations of his life. It is true that the Bible contains variations in its hope for the coming of the kingdom of God. It presents more than one view both of the nature of the kingdom and the agent and means of its coming. But the writers of the two covenants are unified in understanding messianism as an attitude toward history in which the hope for an ideal rule and order of God is seen as having political relevance for this world and its future. To point to a Messiah was to point to the new man. It was to define the shape of a new humanity which is to originate in our history. The messianic ingredient of the Judeo-Christian tradition has bequeathed to us a religion of historical redemption rather than a salvation cult designed primarily to save individuals from an evil world.

This messianism finds a basis in the Old Testament doctrine of creation, with its strong affirmations of the intended goodness of the world. It was a part of the rejection of the fatalistic world views of the static gods of agrarian culture. Since in this Hebraic perspective reality is dynamic, there must be an openness to the coming of the new in history. This coming is seen in the important paradigm of the Exodus event, which involved liberation from political and economic slavery. Though biblical writers point to God's judgment when human egoism stifles the hope, they repeatedly affirm the promise of the coming of the kingdom. The close identity of the themes of redemption and salvation with these worldly hopes forms the biblical basis for current expressions of political theology. Among Roman Catholics Johannes B. Metz has espoused such a theology in an attempt to reverse the strong "privatizing" tendencies of his tradition. Metz summarizes his understanding of the biblical message in this way:

> It stresses that the salvation proclaimed by Jesus is permanently concerned with the world, not in the natural cosmological sense, but in the social and political sense, as the discerning and liberating element of this social world and historical process. The eschatological promises of the biblical tradition—freedom, peace, justice, reconciliation—cannot be reduced to a private matter.[4]

The Old Testament word for peace, *shalom*, often is appropriated as a synonym for "salvation" by the biblical writers. It is at once peace, integrity, community, harmony, wholeness, social righteousness, and justice.

In this context, the affirmation that Jesus is the Christ or Messiah acquires political significance. In a recent paper on "The Possibility of a Messianic Ethic," John Howard Yoder effectively repudiates the commonly held assumption that Jesus did not have a social ethic and that his ethic was limited to a spiritual, personal, rural, or temporary form, applicable only to his own situation.[5] Yoder finds in the New Testament a presentation of Jesus as the bearer of new possibilities for human, social, and political relationships. Such a view undercuts those common ways of doing Christian ethics which concentrate on formulating relevant and responsible decisions based primarily on common sense, pragmatic calculation, or natural law. Most ethicists have assumed that all we can derive from the New Testament are such general concepts as love, faith, and freedom. A messianic interpretation, however, attaches greater relevance to the stance and teachings of Jesus as a political figure.

The revered song of Mary, the Magnificat, contains revolutionary utterances in its descriptions of the mission of the Messiah who was to come:

> He has shown strength with his arm,
> He has scattered the proud in the imagination of their hearts,
> He has put down the mighty from their thrones,
> And exalted those of low degree;
> He has filled the hungry with good things,
> And the rich he has sent away empty. (Luke 1:51-53)

A few verses later, the birth of John, which is intimately associated with the coming of the Messiah, is explained in a similarly messianic vein. Zechariah announces the redemption of God's people in the political language of being "saved from our enemies, and from the hand of all who hate us" (Luke 1:71). Jesus' ordination for ministry through his baptism by this same John was accompanied by messianic phrases, as he was commissioned the fulfiller of God's promises to Israel (see Luke 3:22 and Isa. 42:1). And the temptations have generally been recognized as being socio-political in nature. Jesus had to decide on the fundamental nature of his mission. As pictured by the Evangelists, Jesus, unlike most middle-class Christians but like his Zealot contemporaries, was very much tempted by the possibilities of leading an insurrection in order to establish his kingship in a nationalistic state.

That he did not choose to fight for a literal Jewish kingdom did not, however, deprive his message of messianic content. His inaugural announcement that the "kingdom of God is at hand" was replete with political connotations for his listeners. The kingdom which Jesus proclaimed is not simply bliss for the spirit of man, but concretely peace, freedom, bread, and justice for the poor of this world. This is especially indicated in his first speech in the synagogue of his home town:

> The Spirit of the Lord is upon me,
> because he has anointed me to preach good news to the poor.
> He has sent me to proclaim release to the captives
> and recovering of sight to the blind,
> to set at liberty those who are oppressed,
> to proclaim the acceptable year of the Lord. (Luke 4:18-19)

This passage is lifted from the messianic framework of Isaiah 61, which Jesus appropriated to state the messianic expectation in social and political terms. There are many Old Testament scholars who identify "the acceptable year of Yahweh" with the Jubilee Year. This was no doubt the association which would have been made by the audience at Nazareth. The Jubilee Year was that fiftieth year when the economic debts and inequities accumulated through the years would be cancelled. If one does not discern the revolutionary impact of such a proclamation, imagine what might happen to any contemporary preacher who would propose to his home congregation sweeping economic realignments that would involve starting from scratch and redistributing property on an equal basis.

In this messianic framework, the cross can be seen as a political alternative to both Zealot insurrection and Essene quietism. It becomes a revolutionary reality; for it is seen as God's way of overcoming evil in the world. John Howard Yoder has observed that the way of the cross is the one area in which the New Testament writers advocate imitating the Messiah. They do not advise a Franciscan mimicking of Jesus' life style. When Paul appealed for celibacy, he did not attempt to buttress his argument by pointing to the example of Jesus. But many passages do call for taking up the cross as a manifestation of Christian discipleship. The believer's cross takes on a social dimension in the context of the messianic nature of the message of the early community. It does not refer to every kind of sickness, suffering, or tension which afflicts Christians. Rather, the believer's cross is the price of the nonconformity that comes in representing to an unwilling world the way of the kingdom which is to come. It constitutes a truly revolutionary way in renouncing both violence and the unjust existing order. This way suffers with the world, yet not as a passive victim, but in loving resistance and love made possible by hope in the reality of the resurrection. Because he believes in the resurrection, the Christian knows that the powers have been defeated. Man is freed from the domination of the structures of government, class, race, and background so as to be able to appropriate the new era in the midst of the old structures for the sake of their transformation.

These messianic motifs are not antithetical to a Pauline view of history which speaks of death and resurrection or to the cosmic christological passages found in the early sections of Philippians, Colossians, and Ephesians. The declaration of the triumph of Christ over the powers and principalities and the assertion of his lordship over all the world may point to a new way to define high and low Christology. Whereas high Christology has been defined in terms of how many propositional affirmations one makes about Christ, there is implicit in these passages a possibility of defining high Christology in terms of how many areas of life are permeated by the lordship of Christ. This may reverse many common judgments. A Billy Graham who has written that he has attempted to keep clear of the moral implications of the Vietnam situation, could be judged in this instance to have a low Christology because of his segregation of a major issue from the purview of the lordship of Christ. On the other hand, some who may not be able to dogmatize their faith may in reality have a high Christology because of their willingness to allow the lordship of Christ to dominate increasing areas of their lives.

APOSTOLIC APOCALYPTIC AGE

The revolutionary consciousness of the first century both fed upon and nourished an apocalyptic view of history. For this reason descriptions of the messianic nature of the New Testament message cannot be fully understood apart from this world view. Since the emergence of the apocalyptic literature represented a most significant development within the Judaism of the inter-testamental period, the early Christian preachers may have uniquely combined apocalyptic teachings and symbols with the older prophetic tradition. Thus, presenting the Jewish messianic figure in servant and universal terms may not have been the anomaly depicted by Brandon.

The bulk of the apocalyptic literature was written from the years 200 B.C. to A.D. 100, the period of Jewish nationalism and the struggle for freedom. The apocalyptic elements in Christianity represent, then, an integral part of the tradition of an illicit religion, struggling to survive against the established order. These writers incarnated the response of faith during terrible days. The origins of this literature may be traced to the Hasidim, the "pious ones," who were zealous supporters of the Maccabees during the time when Antiochus IV Epiphanes (175-163 B.C.) was deter-mined to exterminate the Jewish religion. One of these Hasidim wrote the Book of Daniel, which constitutes "a great affirmation of faith in the overruling purpose of God which could not and would not be frustrated by the devices of evil men. . . ."[6] Al-though both the Essene and the Pharisaic movements may have evolved from the Hasidim, the apocalyptic writers were not representative of any one party but were found over a wide spectrum of Jewish life. Their opposition to the Hellenization of Judaism did not keep them from appropriating alien thoughts and imagery, especially from Greece and Persia.

In a recent study, Graydon F. Snyder helps define, theologi-cally, the nature of the apocalyptic motif in the Bible:

> The heart of biblical apocalyptic theology is what we might call "radically disjunctive eschatology." It affirms the absolute validity of God's promise to mankind through Israel and the historical locus of its fulfillment, yet it denies that present history, or the present institutions of man could lead to that fulfillment.[7]

Here is an attitude of despair combined with a theology of hope, a pessimism about the present held concurrently with an optimism about the end. Because of the bleakness of the time, the candle of hope seemed to burn more brightly. For the apocalyptic view of history defies current frustration in pointing to an unseen goal which gives meaning to the present time. It is an "about-to-be-realized" eschatology in which the immediate future begins to break into the present. Because of the deep conviction that the righteousness of God will at last be vindicated, this theology unites eschatology with social ethics. Apocalypse, which means revelation, foretells through myth the victory of the coming age over the present age of darkness.

Because of similar themes, the apocalyptic motifs are often compared with their prophetic antecedents. Whereas at the turn of the first millennium B.C., the prophets began to communicate the myth through historical narratives, by the third century B.C. the apocalypticists were interpreting history mythologically. Some authorities on this period such as Stanley Brice Frost see the shift as having resulted from the failure of the events of history to verify the prophetic faith in the divine purpose in history itself. The inability of the religious leaders to explain the plight of Israel in the chaos of post-exilic times dealt a severe blow to the belief that history could reveal the divine purpose. Thus, according to this view, *Heilsgeschichte* (salvation history), representing the views of the prophets, gave way to a less teleological view of history. A teleology which looked for a purposeful history was replaced in the apocalyptic by an eschatology which pointed to a purpose beyond history which nevertheless impinged on history. Foster's summary of this position is instructive:

> The apocalyptists are in fact a school of biblical writers who recognized that the burden which Hebrew religion had laid upon history was greater than it could bear. They therefore returned from history to myth, myth in a new amalgam with history, which we have learned to call eschatology. In so doing, however, they abandoned the teleological view of history and with it the attempt to justify in mundane events the ways of God to man.[8]

Other authorities, however, do not find such discontinuity

between the prophetic and the apocalyptic. C. Vriezen, for example, traces a gradual transition from prophecy to eschatology. He recognizes the crisis which came with the failure of history, but he does not see this as a new phenomenon in Jewish history. Foreshadowing the two aeons of the apocalypticists, the prophets discerned two types of Israel, Israel as an empirical people that perishes and Israel as the people of God who remain visible only through the eye of faith:

> Isaiah is the man who on the one hand is certain that Israel (Judah) is no longer of any value as a people in his days and will perish, but who on the other hand firmly believes in the future of his people, because he knows that God is at work on Israel. And therefore his faith gives him the certainty that God will create something new from the coming destruction and chaos: a kingdom of right and justice under a divine kingship, the kingdom of God among mankind, beginning in Israel, but a blessing for the whole world at all times.[9]

Deutero-Isaiah, according to Vriezen, was an even more eschatological preacher; for this later prophet anticipated a salvation for Israel which far transcended an ordinary event. Israel's redemption would be caused by forces beyond history, though the new creation arising from the destruction would come about within the framework of history.

Is such a view entirely inconsistent with the alleged otherworldliness of the apocalyptic writers? New Testament scholars such as Graydon Snyder believe not. The radically disjunctive eschatology of the apocalyptic writers may be regarded as transcendent in the sense of emphasizing the divine action. It is not transcendent, however, in the sense of salvation's taking place in another world. "It is merely the affirmation that the eschatological pull calls for newness rather than structural continuity."[10] Given these similarities, the main difference between these two literatures may have been in style. The apocalyptic message was clothed in pictorial images, fantastic symbolism, and cosmic visions, while the older prophetic themes were presented in the narrative form of promise and fulfillment, judgment and redemption, and deliverance in the age to come. Although biblical scholars do not agree on the extent of the similarity between the prophetic and apocalyptic theology, they do agree on the revolutionary implications of the radical expectation that the new will break into history.

Albert Schweitzer's portrayal of the true Jesus of history as an apocalyptist may be vindicated as scholars increasingly focus on the apocalyptic elements and context of apostolic literature. Jesus' message, including his teachings of the Jubilee Year, and his designation as the Son of Man point to a radically disjunctive eschatology. Such wisdom teachings as "blessed are the poor in spirit" are combined with apocalyptic expectations concerning the kingdom of God. The collection of teachings known as the Sermon on the Mount may well have been understood in a messianic framework. This new community which had begun to live in the Way of the new age gradually came to interpret the Son of Man apocalyptically through their own experience of the radical newness which had come through death and resurrection.

In his article on the apocalyptic form in the New Testament church, Graydon Snyder convincingly documents his thesis that Paul preached a radical disjunction between law and wisdom. But as Snyder goes on to emphasize, Paul in his message to the Corinthians also attacked the perversions of freedom with which the men of Corinth destroyed brotherhood. The radical apocalypticism that enabled Paul to assert, "All things are lawful for me" (1 Cor. 7:12), was misinterpreted by the Corinthians to mean that they were free to eat any kind of meat, offend the brethren through dress, and babble without edification. Paul attempted to maintain his apocalyptic disjunctive and at the same time inform the Corinthians that they were not beyond the discipline and structure of the community. For freedom at the expense of community is self-destruction. Snyder adds that the Corinthian error probably resulted from a Hellenistic tendency to literalize the apocalyptic by interpreting it dualistically in terms of flesh and spirit. The myth became cosmology. Another mistake in interpreting the apocalyptic, according to Snyder, occurred at Thessalonica. There the apocalyptic was literalized chronologically. The myth became history as the people stopped working and simply waited for the coming of the kingdom. "The problem of the delay of the parousia is a problem only in so far as the early community misunderstood and literalized the apocalyptic form."[11]

ATOMIC APOCALYPTIC AGE

In many ways the apocalyptic myth of the end is an accurate picture of our contemporary situation. We live at a time when many signs suggest a world moving toward death. For Christians the apocalyptic mood is gaining ground over Constantinianism. There is a growing consciousness that we have reached the end of a cultural era. Many intellectuals labeled the apocalyptic preachers of earlier generations crackpots or religious fanatics. Now our most radical apocalyptists are eminent scientists warning of the possible end of the world as we know it. Life can be extinguished by overpopulation, the poisoning of the atmosphere, the nuclear holocaust. This apocalypticism places the future as the burden of all mankind. There are two ways. Either we will gain a new future in a common struggle or we will lose all in a common annihilation. Technology will either become the great servant of mankind or the demonic destroyer. There are two worlds. Either we will choose to live in the new age or we will pass away with the old. Since we are unable to find easy remedies for our ailing structures, since we lack the will to change our false priorities, since we can no longer believe in the progressive amelioration of our society, we can only look with hope to the death of old structures and the birth of new ways, goals, institutions, and dreams. We must anticipate a new history under God. Though the social order does not stand open to the future, we look for a radical judgment that will break it open anew. Though we are destined to live in disillusioning, suffering, and cataclysmic times, we can live in the expectation of the radical coming of the new. Hope is not turning one's back on a realistic analysis of the facts; but hope is refusing to accept them as the final course of judgment. The radical Christian should be able to live and hope in spite of present frustration because of his faith in the ultimate victory of the kingdom of righteousness. Those who know a disjunctive eschatology with a faith in the future of God can begin to live in the new era in the midst of the decaying of the old. Revolutionary fervor originates in such hope.

Rediscovering the nature of biblical eschatology can save us from some of the pitfalls of alternative philosophies of history. One such philosophy is *reformism*, derived from a faith in the smooth working of God through history and its secular counterpart, the doctrine of progress. This view is represented by the optimistic sociologist whose faith requires him to marshall evidence of progress even in the face of contrary data. It is also represented by Christians who are anxious if they do not discern a causal relationship between their activity and the Christianization of the world. Because of his basic faith in the reformability of basic institutions, the liberal reformer of one generation will likely become the conservative defender of the status quo in the next. He refuses to consider challenges to the very nature of institutions. He often lowers his sights in the interest of immediate minor reforms. Apocalypticism can offer some valid correctives to this view of history. It can demonstrate that though some institutions may need to be reformed, there are times when new institutions need to arise. There may be those moments when God wills the death of the old in order to effect the birth of the new.

In sharp contrast to the philosophy of reformism, is the spirit of *escapism* and *despair*. When history fails and destroys faith in God's providence or man's upward evolution, there is the tendency to give up and retreat to one's own community or to mystical, meditative efforts to establish a relationship with the transcendent. Such an outlook is poignantly reflected in Richard Rubenstein's *After Auschwitz*. [12] For Rubenstein the genocide of six million Jews in the death camps of Nazi Germany was a *kairos* event of such proportions as to require a fundamental change in

Jewish theology. Because Auschwitz represents the ultimate in irrational evil, Rubenstein can no longer affirm the rationalistic and humanistic view of society that has characterized Jewish liberalism or the *Heilsgeschichte* of Jewish tradition. Rejecting both the myth that the Jews are the chosen people and the myth that God is the Lord of history, he concludes that what is left is the solidarity of a people in the face of tragedy. In this way he moves to an espousal of cultic and ritualistic practices. While one cannot easily refute this position, one can through appropriating the world view of Daniel and Jewish apocalypticism point to the phoenix of hope rising from the ashes of the holocaust without needing to formulate a logical theodicy for the present situation. This need not be entirely a leap in the dark, for the story of redemption offers paradigms of previous happenings of this nature in mankind's pilgrimage. Biblical images of history do stress discontinuity in depicting redemption as coming from radical judgment, the coming of the new from the death of the old.

Another mistaken alternative to the biblical apocalyptic is what might be called a *cosmological literalization.* Those at Corinth who literalized Paul's apocalyptic teaching have a counterpart in those who graphically depict a literal heaven and hell removed from the world. By depositing heaven outside of history, the ethics of the kingdom of heaven can be spiritualized and privatized, and any concrete applications need not be taken seriously on this earth. Likewise, in removing hell from history, one can adjust more easily to the gross injustices of our present system. In thus removing salvation from history, schemes are devised whereby it will be possible to escape this world in order to get to heaven. But exercises in describing the furniture of heaven or in measuring the temperature of hell need the corrective of the biblical apocalyptic literature, in which such imagery points to the struggles of man in history. This historical placement of heaven and hell for the believer does not mean, however, that there is no continuation of historical existence through the gift or denial of eternal life. Neither does the historical focus of redemption deny a personal force beyond history which imparts grace and power within the struggle. It does mean that the New Jerusalem is to come down and dwell with men (Rev. 21:1-4).

A cosmological literalization of the apocalyptic message has often been paralleled or combined with a *chronological literalization,* such as took place at Thessalonica. Here the pictorial language appropriated from Eastern mythological forms to express a philosophy of history is taken as factual history. The Bible is treated as a scientific resource in order to schematize history and predict coming events. In dispensational and premillennial periodization, such events as the coming of the new state of Israel are seen as proofs of the imminent coming of the kingdom. Such setting of dates and seeking of signs runs counter to the admonitions of the biblical writers themselves. Although premillennial and chiliastic preachers have been most discerning in sensing the basic sickness of our civilization long before liberals were shaken from their naive optimism, their emphases conflict at some points with the basic thrusts of the apocalyptic message. Scholars who have read back such a literalization into the life of the early community, can easily dismiss the eschatological ethics as "interim ethics" because they were constructed on the belief that the kingdom would come soon. Premillennialists, on the other hand, can futurize the message and maintain that the revolutionary and messianic teachings of Jesus are not meant to be lived until Jesus comes and begins his reign. Biblical apocalypticism, however, sees the kingdom neither as completely accomplished nor as existing completely in the future. Rather, the kingdom is the future breaking into the present. As heaven cannot be removed from history, neither can it be removed entirely from the present. For the radical Christian, eternal life, heaven, the kingdom, should begin now. In Christ one begins to be a part of the new creation. The kingdom is not to be erected, spiritualized, or schematized; it is to be lived.

Another mistaken alternative to the biblical apocalyptic— perhaps a secularized brand of the literalization of the millennial kingdom—is *utopianism.* Of all of the perversions of the apocalyptic world view, utopianism is the one noted most often by critics of revolutionary movements. Utopianism refers to the temptation of freedom and revolutionary movements to absolutize their own party, activity, or revolution. This lack of self-criticism has often led to a self-righteous intolerance which denies the very human rights originally sought. Because of this phenomenon, critics have cited the need for an attitude espousing permanent revolution. The biblical apocalyptic disjunctive demands a recurring death of the old and birth of the new.

In its hope for the future, Marxism has represented precisely a worldly utopian version of messianic visions of peace and justice. In the context of the Marxist-Christian dialogue, Ernst Bloch has enthusiastically noted Marxism's indebtedness to the biblical horizons of future and hope. As a Marxist, however, he wishes to secularize the dimension of hope by dismissing the transcendence of grace as envisaged in biblical eschatology. Jan Lochman from the Christian side answers that in denying the Creator of the world, the Marxist comes to regard the world as the ultimate source of meaning. This leads to the pitfall of divinizing man and the movement of history itself. Lochman believes that the problem with atheist interpretation is that it is not secular enough. It is in adhering to that which is beyond history working in history that the Christian vision of the world is able to avoid absolutizing the historical. That is its defense against utopianism. Lochman develops this position well:

> The transcendence of grace as breaking the ontocratic structures means a radical freedom in the secular realm. The world in which we live is not the Ultimate. It is a penultimate reality. Human action is a secular activity and it's not the soteriological act, the process of self-redemption. In the biblical conception man is not burdened with a soteriological mission. He does not have to perform this "mission impossible.". . .he is very much engaged in an effort to build a human secular city. In this he is asked to deploy all his energy because the new Jerusalem is not the tower of Babel. We need not climb into the heaven. We may remain where we are, that means, on the earth. The new Jerusalem is coming down.[13]

To the danger of absolutizing human activity and to the tragic totalitarianism of messianic claims, the biblical view, which neither worships history or negates the world, offers a needed corrective. The vision of a God who pulls from ahead should free Christians from fatalism and utopianism and release them for permanent revolutionary activity.

CHAPTER VII

Strategies for a Revolution of Hope

To identify with Jesus is to identify with a revolutionary personage. To accept him as the Messiah or Christ is to believe in a kingdom of justice, righteousness, and love. To have a biblical eschatological perspective is to have a revolutionary consciousness. To appropriate the apocalyptic mood of the Bible is to feel at times that there must be a sharp break with the past in our own lives and institutions. In the sense of personal conversion, evangelistic strategists have recognized that Christianity is always within one generation of extinction. Concerning basic institutions, however, Christians have largely assumed that change will occur only gradually through updated methods, adaptations to various pressures, and fresh leadership from time to time.

The biblical apocalyptic view is gaining ground on the evolutionary outlook. But the change this requires is far more radical than many of us could possibly have envisioned during the economic and ecclesiastical boom of the postwar period of the forties and fifties. Since the direction of American life was viewed by most ecclesiastical and political liberals as basically right, it was felt that social problems could be corrected by simple repairs in the malfunctioning of the machinery. It has been the growing disillusionment with such faith that has provided a strong catalyst for the growth of radicalism both within and outside the church. Many youth discerned that the ideals and sincere efforts of their parents did not seem to dent the corrupt social structures. More cynically, these youth came to feel that such ideals were often a smoke screen behind which oppression and corruption were hid. Some pragmatic liberals, who repudiated utopianism a decade or so ago in their desire to be effectively relevant, now appear to be quite utopian in their assumption that America will make the necessary adjustments without basic changes in its institutions or directions. The liberal is one who feels that an old-style colonial war is a mistake; the radical believes it to be a logical expression of economic and military policies that are worldwide. Richard Shaull offers a similar analysis:

> If the danger of the radical is to "present impossibilities as possibilities," the crisis of liberalism is its limiting of the possibilities so that we have no clear way ahead. Thus the liberal ends up with his own strange brand of utopianism: the expectation that the present system can provide solutions of which it is incapable.[1]

Earlier in this century, a disillusionment with an optimistic faith in man led liberal theologians to rediscover the doctrine of sin. Since, according to this neoorthodox analysis, the fundamental problem was in man himself, the cure could not be found in man but only beyond him in God's revelation and activity. Something analogous may be happening today. If society with its false priorities, its racism, and its militarism is basically sick, then salvation will not come either through natural evolution (the hope of liberalism) or through a penetration of structures by Christian men of action (the hope of secular theology). Something else is needed. The sick structures can be saved only by something outside, the apocalyptic vision of God's pulling men to live in the real and new age, the forming of new communities of men who are beginning to feel liberated from the corrupt institutions of the present.

Since the Christian radical does not believe in relinquishing his responsibility to participate in God's redeeming activity in the world, he is searching for new paradigms, is testing new strategies, and is open to new forms of Christian witness and action. If his stance is truly radical, he will be aware that any new structures which may emerge to challenge the old will also be subject to the

125

sins of collective greed and pride. Nevertheless, he does not despair, for he has hope that by the grace of God something new will emerge out of the collapse of the old. Thus he seeks and responds to new forms of living, witness, and strategy. The initial struggles with some of these strategies or life styles will be examined in the context of the perspective of radical faith.

PARABOLIC ACTS OR PRUDENTIAL TACTICS

The accusation that radicals combine an abundance of moral absolutism with a dearth of constructive programs is mirrored in some ways in the genuine philosophical struggle about the nature of action itself. To some extent this struggle might be defined as between an ethic of promise and an ethic of calculation. Liberal strategy was most often characterized by a prudential calculation of potential results in relation to efforts to Christianize society or to make the world a better place. While not entirely lacking in such pragmatic concerns, radical action has tended toward confrontation, parabolic acts, and eschatological ethics.

The ship *Phoenix* sailed toward the port of Haiphong, loaded with medical supplies from the Peace Movement in the very country which was bombing North Vietnam. Its mission did not represent any grand strategy to bring the war to an end. Rather it served both as a prophetic act judging the destructive action taking place and as a parabolic sign pointing to the brotherhood that should exist between the two peoples. A minister interviewed on a talk show was pressed about his role in a demonstration: "Do you not realize that the negative backlash this produced far outweighed any good you may have accomplished?" In reply he said simply that he had acted as he did because he felt compelled to witness to his understanding of the Christian faith. Presenting bread to congressmen during the Poor People's campaign, placing in coffins the names of those who had died in battle, serving communion at Lincoln Park during the Democratic National Convention, and conducting masses in the Pentagon represent but a few of the many modern counterparts to the prophetic signs reported in the biblical narratives.

The truth of the matter is that any calculation of the consequences is made difficult by the unpredictability of the "happening" and the response of the Establishment. Often two very contradictory results may be measured. A visible action on the part of radical Blacks may produce a vigorous backlash. But while the action alienates some, it may pull others to a more humane position. For example, in the Chicago area following a particular disruption of Blacks, some voices which had once charged that "Martin Luther King was a Communist" began asking "Why don't the Blacks follow the teachings of Martin Luther King?" On several occasions I myself have been involved in acts of witness which I feared would bring more misunderstanding than good. To my surprise, however, there often have emerged beautiful and unexpected responses.

In more theological terms, we can affirm that since no one can predict accurately the result of his actions, he needs to be faithful to what he believes is right and leave the results to the working of the Holy Spirit. The Christian radical does not understand his own actions prudentially. He is not obliged to demonstrate the pragmatic feasibility of all of his actions because he is freed by his confidence in the present and future reality of God's kingdom to formulate ethical responses based on the righteousness of this kingdom.

The current rediscovery of the prophetic No and Woe is a departure from a previous consensus which taught us to accent the positive and eliminate the negative. Whereas my youthful generation was pleased when the Establishment granted exemption from ROTC on the grounds of conscience, contemporary radicals utter a resounding No to militarization itself as being inimical to liberal education. The radical No can be a valid witness to the Yes because implied in the No is often a radical Yes. A No directed against war has been one of the strongest ways of saying Yes for peace. A resounding No to injustice often constitutes a Yes to the vision of justice. The No which is exalted in the apocalyptic book of Daniel is contained within the framework of a radical expression of hope. A No to a sick society through a stance of nonconformity should point to a passionate Yes to the vision of a new order.

RECONCILIATION OR CONFRONTATION

The Yes and the No of radical witness is closely related to the tension existing between the traditional concern for Christian reconciliation and the current propensity for prophetic confrontation. Is it possible for Christians to be both peacemakers and prophets at the same time? Whereas it is true that the radical mood often degenerates into frustrated hatred, the liberal tendency has been to avoid confrontation in order to keep the peace. This strategy of reconciliation has often tolerated the injustices borne by the dispossessed in order to avoid disturbing the possessors. Liberal strategy has generally espoused a neutrality in which the church acts as a third party providing a neutral platform for the reconciliation of opposing interests. Increasingly, radical Christians are coming to feel that such neutrality embodies an ecclesiastical triumphalism which assumes that the church can objectively live above the scenes of human struggle. On the contrary, since the biblical bias is definitely on the side of the poor and dispossessed, the Christian must be *in* the struggle, though at some points not of it. Jürgen Moltmann maintains that "The goal of Christian universalism can be realized precisely through the dialectic of siding with the humiliated."[2]

Consistent with its neutrality, liberalism has more often tried to adjust the alienated to a sick society than participate with the outcasts in challenging false establishment values. This "band-aid" approach attempts to minister to the symptoms of social illness instead of prophetically attacking the causes. Yet, the radical may easily overreact to this liberal temptation and forget that acts of mercy and ministry to basic human needs have always been the legacy of fundamental Christianity. This servant role need not undermine prophetic responsibility; often it is precisely through putting on band-aids that Christians are led to probe the sources of the infection.

128

At times the radical has been attempting to reapply the biblical truth that reconciliation can come through confrontation. The pericope about Jesus' tipping the tables is not antithetical to his designation as the Prince of Peace. When Martin Luther King led a march through Chicago neighborhoods, he was accused of increasing racial prejudice because of the implied threat to integration. He naturally replied that he did not cause such ugly behavior but that the marches merely brought to the surface the prejudice already there. As long as the Civil Rights struggle remained in the South, most Northerners could maintain that racism was a Southern and not a Northern phenomenon. And as long as this assumption went unchallenged, there was little chance for reconciliation between the races in the North. The racial prejudice had to be exposed before it could be dealt with. An easy integration without a genuine response to alienation is impossible. This is stated well by J. Christian Beker, a contemporary biblical theologian at Princeton:

> The so-called biblical center of reconciliation may not be as central to the New Testament as recent theology has asserted. Reconciliation must pass through the revolution of the cross; and even apart from biblical insights, reconciliation may not be a target-word in our time, since a *bourgeois* affluent Church interprets it inevitably as a sanctioning of the *status quo*. Reconciliation in the race issue has simply been translated as integration. Whereas the Church should have recognized that integration which by-passes "Black Power" demands means a resurrection without a cross.[3]

An appropriate biblical model may be the instructions given in Matthew 18:15-20 on the style of reconciliation. This passage, which immediately precedes the admonition to Peter about unlimited forgiveness, advocates direct confrontation. If a brother sins against you, go and tell him his fault, and if he still does not listen, take others with you. If this still proves to be futile, "tell it to the church" (vs. 17). Here confrontation is presented as an integral part of the act of reconciliation. An easy peace without confrontation is often achieved by keeping the lid on basic injustices. Confrontation apart from the context of reconciliation

129

eventuates in an unending cycle of retaliation. Only peace achieved through confrontation, involving grace and judgment, love and justice, will suffice. If confrontive tactics should be necessary, should they be violent or nonviolent? It is to this difficult problem that we now turn.

VIOLENCE OR NONVIOLENCE

The word "violence" has generally been taken to refer to sudden injury or destruction, but radicals apply the term more widely. Violence occurs when three children are brutally killed in the bombing of a black Birmingham church; but violence also occurs every time another Birmingham child dies from the institutional racism that denies proper medicine, food, and care to large portions of the black community. Violence against people is part of militant guerrilla activity; but it occurs much more extensively in the collusion of the CIA with suppressive regimes. Violence becomes a reality both when demonstrators violate the personal rights of others and when their own human rights to assemble are denied.

The debate over violence has also shifted its focus. From the problem of the legitimacy of supporting the military actions of our government, the crucial question for the radical Christian now is to what extent he can approve of revolutionary counterviolence. Recently, a representative of the liberal Establishment was attempting to argue a young radical out of his pacifism. Eventually the youth replied, "If you really convince me that violence is necessary in order to preserve freedom in other countries, then I will go underground and begin to bomb military installations here or join a guerrilla force in the third world." This unexpected answer prompted the antagonist of pacifism to shake his head and turn away.

Their infatuation with Martin Luther King's early successes in nonviolence having ebbed, radicals are now divided in their basic convictions. Some social action people in the church have ceased to espouse the power of nonviolence and are looking to the possibility of revolutionary violence. Some revolutionary church-men in South America, represented in this country by theologian Richard Shaull, refuse to rule out armed force as a part of Christian action. At the same time, a radical pacifist movement is gaining strength in Roman Catholicism, a movement character-ized both by basic obedience to the nonviolent cross and by bold disruptive challenges to the war machine. And offsetting to some extent the growing militancy of young radicals in the Movement, there remains the influential nonviolent contingent inspired by such pacifists as David Dellinger and Staughton Lynd. At the WCC Conference on Church and Society held at Geneva in 1966, Professor Jan Lochman reported that most of the delegates from the third world approved of revolutionary force because they were well aware of the many kinds of force employed by the great powers to impose injustice. On the other hand, the delegates from the highly industrialized nations, who could more easily afford the luxury of nonviolence, adamantly repudiated vio-lence.[4]

All radical Christians can join in attacking the hypocrisy of a nation's advocating nonviolence for the oppressed and the Blacks while spending billions for weapons of death. The same people who profit personally from the economic suppression backed by the Marines in South America are alarmed when some bricks are thrown through windows at home. The pious admonitions about violence we give to ghetto Blacks and third-world revolutionaries are but another example of finding a splinter in our brother's eye when there is a log in our own. In reality nonviolence is some-thing we can preach to others only insofar as we practice it ourselves. This critique is not, however, limited to the Establish-ment's militarists; we must also abandon what John Pairman Brown has called Establishment Pacifism. This is a pacifism that has been so accepted and praised by the powers that be that its advocates are wooed to become cooperative citizens of the mili-tary state. "Respectable pacifism is novocaine to deaden our awareness of complicity; it's the Establishment's ultimate tech-nique for castrating our resistance."[5] Establishment pacifists are most congenial to their neighbors and fellow church members who have been nonpacifist participants in their nation's wars but are horrified at the nonpacifism of the desperate poor. Such pacifists need to accept the biblical challenge to identify with the concerns of the poor and to seriously question their overidentification with the wealthy and powerful.

Radical Christians who feel that they cannot absolutely rule against all violence in revolutionary struggles do so on the basis of new versions of the just-war theory. Such a formulation was presented in October, 1966, by the theological study group of the Christian Peace Conference. Their document approved the possibility of participating in violent revolutions only as an *ultima ratio*, which means only

> (a) if violent measures have already been used by the oppressors . . .; (b) if all possible methods of legal criticism and legal actions have been courageously and patiently tried, without success; (c) if a situation has arisen which . . . is more harmful to human beings than violent revolution would probably be.[6]

Many have become very sympathetic to the "lesser of two evils" argument. As Reinhold Niebuhr reasoned that armed warfare against Nazi Germany was a lesser evil than fascist tyranny in large portions of the world, so many are coming to believe that in some circumstances an armed resistance and overthrow of repressors may be a lesser evil than the violence which, though bloodless, condemns entire peoples to continual degradation and misery.

Other radicals, however, are certain that such militant apocalypticism is a perversion of the Christian perspective. They believe that it is impossible to fulfill life through death. We "cannot create a new order of justice by murdering all those who supported injustice, for injustice will have merely changed hands."[7] "By fighting the demon with his own weapons, you can demolish the structure he's temporarily living in—at the expense of transferring him to your own address."[8] The violence that liberates can quickly become the violence that enslaves, as history has demonstrated so often. The way that is still more revolutionary than violence may well be the way that repudiates even the methods of the Establishment. Jacques Ellul, French lay theologian and professor of law, offers a unique approach in his book on *Violence*, a position reminiscent of sixteenth-century radicalism. Ellul argues that Christians, who should identify with the struggles of the poor, may condone violence when a man is in despair and sees no other way out because such violence is natural and normal to man. Violence, in fact, is necessary, indispensable, and inevitable to the experience of man. Yet, violence is fundamentally counter to the order of Christ. By grace Christians will not be a part of the natural order. If the Christian's identification with the poor leads to violence, he will know he is doing wrong. According to Ellul, then, Christians, by the grace of God, must radically refuse to justify violence in any circumstance.[9] Ellul especially attacks the current faddism in ecumenical circles that tends to sanction and even idealize revolutionary violence.

Radicals who repudiate both an Establishment Pacifism and revolutionary counter-violence may wish to opt for a revolutionary strategy of loving resistance. Ellul speaks of such resistance as the violence of love. As he defines it, such loving violence is that battle against injustice, oppression, and authoritarianism which is waged with prayer, the Word of God, the justice of God, and the zeal imparted by the gospel of peace. This kind of love can evoke much trouble if it is affirmed, lived, and attested by gentle signs.[10] For whites it might involve teaching the high priority of nonviolence to white policemen, the national guard, and the military establishment. Lochman's admonition is sound:

> ...the testimony of non-violent love is not true if it is understood quietistically or ideologically (as a luxury-attitude...); it is true only if it is expressed in serious Christian testimony, i.e., in a revolutionary way, attacking the inhuman, godless structures of the world in the light of God's Kingdom. It is only through ecumenical solidarity with the hungry, oppressed people in the developing countries, and by supporting their justified revolutionary demands, that the privileged Christians of Europe [and America] today can make a testimony of non-violent love which will carry any conviction.[11]

Ellul cites three conditions that must be met by any use of spiritual violence ("loving resistance" may be a less confusing term). First, such violence, or resistance, must reject human means of gaining victory. Second, it must totally exclude physical or psychological violence. Third, it is based on a faith in the promise of the lordship of Christ over all of life and in a belief in the coming of the kingdom through God's action, not ours.[12]

Those of us who espouse some form of revolutionary non-violence will probably fail to avoid tainted motives. We may fail because our affluence grants us the luxury of such an ideology. We may affirm nonviolence as a rationalization for not joining the struggle or as an accommodation to a repressive mood which greatly fears any violence from the oppressed. Yet we may also believe as we do in faithfulness to the revolutionary way of the cross. William Sloane Coffin, Jr., recently said:

> I am afraid we are gradually moving toward the situation where citizens will have to choose between options no citizen should have to confront—namely, between *change* forced by violence and the *repression* of violence forced by no change. To me this means that the marching order for the church should read: twice as nonviolent, and twice as militant.[13]

INDIVIDUAL OR CORPORATE

A current watershed debate in Christendom is over whether the individual or society should be the object of redemption. In coming down strongly on the political side of this debate, the Christian radical nevertheless should never forget the revolutionary implications inherent in the Christian emphasis on the value of each person. Yet, while Christianity does focus on a Person as the clue to the nature of reality, it is significant that the New Testament references to Christ as Savior point to his Saviorhood of all men and of the world rather than support the widespread notion of a personal Savior. Because of the impossibility of individual wholeness without community and the impossibility of true community without authentic individual freedom, the Christian must simultaneously affirm both the individual and the world as the object of God's redeeming activity. The danger of a personal salvation apart from social liberation is stated by Jürgen Moltmann: "If one grasps only the promise of freedom in faith and forgets the realistic demand for the liberation of this world, the gospel becomes the religious basis for the justification of society. . . ."[14]

A more basic debate among Christians involves not so much the object of redemption as the means of redemption. Traditional revivalism has not been without a social passion for the world, but it has assumed that the way to change the world was through the transformation of individual lives. Similarly, some social action liberals have assumed that the primary method of changing the world is through individuals fired with a social passion. Such a belief has often implied a distinction between the moral Christian and the immoral church, as though individual members could and would be more pure in witness than the corporate body could ever hope to be.

Radical Christians advocate that the community of faith become a consensus-forming body for a corporate expression of judgment and redemption to the world. It is true that church congregations have long made many corporate decisions. They have struggled through to a consensus on the pastor's salary, the color of bricks in the new building, the kind of organ needed, the purchasing of additional property for community service. But if one sees the corporate body utilizing all of its encounters to solve these kinds of issues while at the same time avoiding the great public issues plaguing mankind and impinging on the consciences of concerned Christians, then he is justified in supposing that to tackle the truly basic problems of an era one has to get outside the church. Radical Christians are not satisfied with this style. They judge as invalid the common argument that the church cannot deal with controversial issues because the pluralism of the membership leads to impasses and divisiveness. In working through the minutiae mentioned above, congregations have been forced to learn to live in the midst of differences. The radical believes that true community can come only through honest confrontation and that the Spirit can be released in real power only by a witness born of a corporate talking through to consensus. Bringing such a strategy into practice will require some radically new forms of institutional life.

EVOLUTIONARY OR REVOLUTIONARY

The changes demanded in the institutions of our society are not moderate; nor can they evolve gradually over a period of time. It is not enough to adjust institutions or to adjust to them. To feel that the old structures can be reformed is not to deal adequately with a system that continues to oppress peoples in the third world and refuses to meet the needs of the poor at home. For this reason radicals of different varieties think in terms of "guerrilla warfare." Such activity may involve a systematic subversion of institutions in order to bring about a transformation of their nature in spite of themselves. Guerrilla activity may consist of constant pressures from without, demanding small changes at many points in a structure solidified against change. A growing definition of such activity advocates helping to create alternative life styles and structures, such as free universities, as a way to challenge the old and bring in the new. Such is the mood of young radicals who affirm: "We are not called to make a sick world well. We are called to act well. This is a powerful political act itself. It means being the revolution."[15] According to Richard Shaull, the Christian's contribution may be to offer the revolutionary those perspectives from the faith "which free him to break the bonds of the secular, empirical ethos, dream new dreams about the future of man, and cultivate the creative imagination so as to be capable of thinking about new problems in new ways, and defining new goals and models for a new society."[16]

Does the analogy of "guerrilla warfare" have any application to the institutional life of the church itself? Is the locus for the Christian radical inside or outside the church? Many Christians who have given up hope for effective witness in many power structures are nevertheless still moving within the orbit of the church because of the relatively greater democracy, pluralism, and flexibility which remain there. The militant radical demands on the churches are a compliment of a kind, since the radicals thereby judge the church to be more open to change than many other human institutions. Revolutionary activity does not arise in places of complete despair—it emerges where there is a glimmer of hope. The freedom to form ad hoc groups and still remain within the larger institutional framework of the church has offered radical Christians a base for witness both within and without the church. Even many of those who have been forced outside the institutional church nevertheless refuse to end their dialogue concerning the radical vocation of the faith. In assemblies, synods, and conventions, and in a variety of ways and attitudes, radical Christians are confronting the church about its true nature and witness.

Like their secular counterparts, many Christian radicals feel that the place to be is in creating new structures to replace the ones which are dying. Underground churches, the name bearing the analogy to guerrilla movements, are being formed. Some are adopting sectarian models. Anomalously, Richard Shaull, who is Professor of Ecumenics at Princeton Theological Seminary, suggests that "The time has come when we must rediscover—in church and society—the meaning of our sectarian heritage."[17] Rosemary Ruether, a Roman Catholic theologian, has called for much the same thing. Feeling that the dreams which surfaced with Vatican II will not be voluntarily implemented by the hierarchy but must be forced upon them by underground and para-institutional groups, she advocates a free church movement for her own tradition.

> The free church, in the sense that I am using it, is the free community within historical Christianity. It is founded on a view of the church which denies that hierarchical institutionalization belongs to the essence of the church. The church is seen essentially as the gathered community of explicit believers in which sacramental distinctions between clergy and laity are abolished, priestly roles become purely contextual and functional; the whole community

137

arising by joint covenant entered into by the existential analogue of believer's baptism; that is to say, by voluntary adult decision. This concept of the believer's church is, I believe, the authentic church, and it is the understanding of the church which ever reappears in the avant garde at the moments of real church renewal.[18]

These authentic democratic expressions of the church springing from a hunger for community and a desire for witness cannot replace the institutional church, which for Ruether remains as a secondary form of the church. In her view, the institutional church is needed to perpetuate the church's tradition in order to keep the gospel available to each new generation. "The historical church . . . remains vital and is constantly renewed through its ability to take in and absorb the insights of the believer's church."[19]

Whether it consists of guerrilla activity within, *ecclesiolae in ecclesia* (small fellowships within the church), or new structures outside, the radical church may be defined as any disciplined community of love which forms under the lordship of Christ for witness to the coming of the kingdom. This corresponds with Emil Brunner's ecclesiology, which maintains that the church in the biblical sense is a fellowship rather than an institution.[20] This is not to spiritualize the doctrine of the community in mission. A fellowship in which people live and love and serve is far more visible than the organizational charts of bureaucratic Christendom.

The ecumenical movement may likewise require redefinition from a radical perspective. Since the Greek meaning of the word "ecumenical" implies the relationship of the total people of God to the entire world, ecumenism cannot be thought of as limited to Christians coming together for fellowship or consensus-making. Ecumenicity entails more than movements toward ecclesiastical merger or conciliar activity. It points to the whole world as God's sphere of activity, an activity in which the church is commissioned to participate. By such a redefinition the ecumenical movement can be seen in the Peace and Freedom Movement and in all the struggles for justice and peace in our time. Not that the church is to be identified with the Peace and Freedom Movement. Christian cadres, fellowships, and congregations which meet for celebration and formulation of their faith will be consciously Christian in their orientation. But the broader Peace and Freedom Movement will likely form a major context for the church's ecumenical activity. This radical definition of the church as being present wherever a small fellowship gathers in the way of Jesus for mission is a more particularistic definition of the church than is generally given. On the other hand, the view of ecumenicity as encompassing the presence of the church in all the struggles for the coming of justice and peace is far more inclusive than the usual understanding. This is consistent with our view of radical as rooted in the particular and manifested in the revolutionary.

To be a Christian is to be a radical. It is to probe the roots of the faith so as to tap its power and reality. The radical Christian will not be anti-theological; he will be able to articulate in some ways the reason for the hope which lies within him. To be a Christian is to experience death and resurrection, to know the death of the old and the birth of the new. To be a Christian, therefore, is to become a revolutionary of a kind. One's theology will be translated into activity and take shape in counter life styles. "To be a Christian is to be an extremist." Moderation is a Greek ideal more than a Christian teaching. "Christian faith is not a half-way measure; it talks about going two miles instead of one, of plucking out the eyes that disturb, of dying on a cross."[21]

To be a radical Christian is to bring the revolutionary foundation of Christianity to all movements for change and freedom and to point to Christianity's revolutionary implications. To be a radical Christian may be to follow the loving Christ in the midst of revolution and to call on the revolutionary Christ to disturb counter-revolutionary attitudes. By witness and example, it will involve Christianizing the revolution and radicalizing Christians. It will proclaim the utopian nature of the kingdom without imbibing a utopianism which sees one's own particular movement or program as ultimate. God's judgment will be pronounced on evil men and structures in such a way that the same judgment will fall upon the radical Christian himself. Being a radical Christian may mean being classified as cop-outs by the Zealots and as Zealots by the Establishment. It may mean following the way of suffering love in the revolution and being persecuted by the Establishment for violent revolutionary activity. It will involve being *in* the revolution but in some ways not *of* it. Above all, the Christian radical, by God's help, will point to and take on revolutionary faith, revolutionary hope, and revolutionary love. He will not claim this revolutionary power for himself. If such power is present, it will be welcomed as a gift and as the first fruit of God's revolutionary kingdom.

Notes

Chapter I

[1] Jürgen Moltmann, *Religion, Revolution, and the Future,* tr. by Douglas Meeks (New York: Scribner's, 1969), p. 134.

[2] See Gordon Kaufman, *Systematic Theology: A Historicist Perspective* (New York: Scribner's, 1968) for a full explication of this position.

[3] Moltmann, *Religion, Revolution, and the Future,* pp. 9-10.

[4] John A. T. Robinson, "Not Radical Enough?" *The Christian Century,* LXXXVI (Nov. 12, 1969), 1446.

[5] Bruce O. Boston, "How are Revelation and Revolution Related?" *Theology Today,* XXVI (July, 1969), 144.

[6] John Pairman Brown, *The Liberated Zone: A Guide to Christian Resistance* (Richmond, Virginia: Knox, 1969), p. 40.

[7] Peter Berger, "Between Tyranny and Chaos," *The Christian Century,* LXXXV (Oct. 30, 1968), 1365-70.

[8] James Douglass, *The Non-Violent Cross: A Theology of Revolution and Peace* (New York: Macmillan, 1968), p. 8.

[9] Paul Lehmann, "Christian Theology in a World in Revolution," *Openings for Marxist-Christian Dialogue,* ed. by Thomas Ogletree (Nashville: Abingdon, 1969), pp. 110-111.

[10] From J. M. Lochman's report, "Ecumenical Theology of Revolution," *New Theology No. 6,* ed. by Martin E. Marty and Dean G. Peerman (Toronto: Macmillan, 1969), p. 105.

[11] Moltmann, *Religion, Revolution, and the Future,* p. 32.

[12] Rolland F. Smith, "A Theology of Rebellion," *New Theology No. 6,* p. 141.

Chapter II

[1] See Rosemary Ruether, "The Free Church Movement in Contemporary Catholicism," *New Theology No. 6,* pp. 284-286.

[2] Richard Shaull, "Christian Faith as Scandal in a Technocratic World," *New Theology No. 6,* p. 132.

3 Walter Klassen, review of "Gewaltlosigkeit im Taüfertum: Eine Untersuchung zur theologischen Ethik des oberdeutschen Täufertums der Reformationszeit," by Clarence Bauman. In *The Mennonite Quarterly Review,* XLIII (Oct. 1969), 334.

4 See Thomas J. J. Altizer, *The Gospel of Christian Atheism* (Philadelphia: Westminster, 1966), p. 9 and pp. 89ff.

5 Moltmann, *Religion, Revolution, and the Future,* p. 25.

6 John Howard Yoder, "The Hermeneutics of the Anabaptists," *The Mennonite Quarterly Review,* XLI (Oct. 1967), 302.

7 For this analysis I am indebted to John Howard Yoder, *ibid.,* p. 301.

8 Hans J. Hillerbrand, "The Anabaptist View of the State," *The Mennonite Quarterly Review,* XXXII (April, 1958), 83-89.

9 *Ibid.,* p. 91.

10 Quoted from Robert Friedmann, "Claus Felbinger's Confession of 1560," *The Mennonite Quarterly Review,* XXIX (April, 1955), 147.

11 Harold S. Bender, "The Anabaptist Vision," *The Recovery of the Anabaptist Vision,* ed. by Guy S. Hershberger (Scottdale, Pa.: Herald, 1957), pp. 42ff.

12 Found in *Great Voices of the Reformation,* ed. by Harry Emerson Fosdick (New York: Random House, 1952), p. 291.

13 Peter Rideman, *Confession of Faith,* tr. by Kathleen Hasenberg (Bungay, Suffolk: Hodder and Stoughton, 1950), p. 87.

14 Markus Barth, "Baptism and Evangelism," *Scottish Journal of Theology,* XII (March, 1959), 32ff.

15 Carl Braaten, *The Future of God* (New York: Harper, 1969), p. 31.

16 Vernard Eller, "Protestant Radicalism," *The Christian Century,* LXXXIV (Nov. 1, 1967), 1391ff.

17 John Howard Yoder, "The Prophetic Dissent of the Anabaptists," *The Recovery of the Anabaptist Vision,* p. 101.

18 Gordon Kaufman, "Nonresistance and Responsibility," *Concern* (Nov., 1958), p. 24.

Chapter III

1 Jan Lochman, "Gospel for Atheists," *Theology Today,* XXVI (Oct., 1969), 299-311.

2 *Ibid.,* p. 305.

3 *Ibid.,* p. 307.

4 *Ibid.,* p. 308.

5 Moltmann, *Religion, Revolution, and the Future,* p. 63.

6 Dietrich Bonhoeffer, *Ethics* (New York: Macmillan, 1961), p. 179.

7 *Ibid.,* p. 180.

8 *Ibid.,* pp. 178-179.

NOTES

9 *Ibid.,* p. 180.

10 Peter Berger, *A Rumour of Angels* (Garden City, N. Y.: Doubleday, 1969).

11 Gordon Kaufman, "On the Meaning of 'God': Transcendence Without Mythology," *Harvard Theological Review,* LIX (April, 1966), 105-132.

12 Richard Shaull, "Theology and the Transformation of Society," *Theology Today,* XXV (April, 1968), 23-36.

13 William Hamilton and Thomas J. J. Altizer, *Radical Theology and the Death of God* (Indianapolis, Ind.: Bobbs-Merrill, 1966), p. xii.

14 Thomas Merton, *Faith and Violence* (South Bend, Indiana: Notre Dame, 1968), p. 260.

15 Paul Van Buren, *The Secular Meaning of the Gospel* (New York: Macmillan, 1963).

16 Herbert Marcuse, *One Dimensional Man* (London: Nicholls, 1968). See Chapter 7, "The Triumph of Positive Thinking: One-Dimensional Philosophy."

17 Dietrich Bonhoeffer, *Act and Being* (New York: Harper, 1961). See especially pages 79-91.

18 Thomas Ogletree, *The Death of God Controversy* (New York: Abingdon, 1966), p. 45.

19 Moltmann, *Religion, Revolution, and the Future,* p. 68.

20 Helmut Gollwitzer, *The Demands of Freedom* (New York: Harper, 1965).

21 Dietrich Bonhoeffer, *The Cost of Discipleship* (New York: Macmillan, 1963), pp. 45-48.

Chapter IV

1 These are descriptive phrases of Christopher Lasch, *The Agony of the American Left* (New York: Vintage, 1969), p. 212.

2 Kenneth Keniston, *Young Radicals* (New York: Harcourt, Brace & World, 1968). See especially Chapter 1.

3 Carl Oglesby, *Let Us Shape the Future* (Chicago: Students for a Democratic Society), p. 5.

4 Jack Newfield, *A Prophetic Minority* (New York: Signet, 1966), p. 20

5 John Gerasis, "Imperialism and Revolution in America," *To Free a Generation,* ed. by David Cooper (New York: Macmillan, 1968), p. 74.

6 Stokely Carmichael, "Black Power," *ibid.,* p. 174.

7 Dotson Rader, *I Ain't Marchin' Anymore* (New York: Paperback Library, 1969), p. 19.

8 *Ibid.,* p. 96.

9 Steve Halliwell, "Personal Liberation and Social Change," *New Politics News,* II (Aug., 1967), 13.

[10] Abbie Hoffman, *Revolution for the Hell of It* (New York: Dial, 1968), p. 62.

[11] Quoted in Newfield, p. 134.

[12] Dietrich Bonhoeffer, *No Rusty Swords* (New York: Harper, 1965), pp. 309-310.

[13] Carl Oglesby, "Democracy is Nothing If It is Not Dangerous," an undated reprint from *The Peacemaker.*

[14] Herbert Marcuse, *An Essay on Liberation* (Boston: Beacon, 1969), pp. 7-8.

[15] Quoted by Lasch, pp. 180-81.

[16] Keniston, p. 37.

[17] *Ibid.,* p. 97.

[18] Marcuse, *One Dimensional Man,* p. 20.

[19] *Ibid.,* p. 27.

[20] Hoffman, p. 68.

[21] R. W. Tucker, "Revolutionary Faithfulness," *New Theology No. 6,* pp. 207-208.

[22] Martin Jezer, "Revolution and Generational Revolt," *Liberation* (July/Aug., 1968), p. 22.

[23] Rader, pp. 159-160.

[24] Jezer, p. 22.

[25] Lasch, p. 188.

[26] Newfield, p. 21.

[27] Quoted from a March 18, 1967 letter to Staughton Lynd, "The Movement: A New Beginning," *Liberation* (May, 1969), p. 12.

[28] Hoffman, p. 70.

[29] Larry Kuenning, "The War Is Over; Letter to Local Board No. 121," Brethren Action Movement Tract 7 (Box 175, North Manchester, Indiana, 1969).

[30] Marcuse, *One Dimensional Man,* p. 66.

[31] Lasch, p. 212.

[32] Tucker, p. 205.

[33] Braaten, p. 29.

[34] Richard Shaull, "Theology and the Transformation of Society," *Theology Today,* XXV (April, 1968), 32.

Chapter V

[1] Charles Hopkins, *Rise of the Social Gospel in American Protestantism, 1865-1915,* XIV, Yale Studies in Religious Education (New Haven, Conn.: 1940), 3.

[2] Walter Rauschenbusch, *A Theology for the Social Gospel* (New York: Abingdon, reprinted 1945), p. 1.

NOTES

[3] Harvey Cox, *The Secular City* (New York: Macmillan, 1965), p. 107.

[4] See articles by David Little and George Younger in *The Secular City Debate,* ed. by Daniel Callahan (New York: Macmillan, 1966), pp. 69-74 and 77-80.

[5] Rauschenbusch, p. 26.

[6] See the section, "The Influence of Sectarianism," in Donovan Smucker, "The Origins of Walter Rauschenbusch's Social Ethics" (unpublished Ph.D. dissertation, University of Chicago, 1957), pp. 80-187.

[7] Jürgen Moltmann, "Toward a Political Hermeneutics of the Gospel," *New Theology No. 6,* p. 87.

[8] Rauschenbusch, pp. 146, 142, 130.

[9] *Ibid.,* p. 73.

[10] *Ibid.,* pp. 198, 204.

[11] *Ibid.,* p. 208.

[12] H. Richard Niebuhr, *The Kingdom of God in America* (New York: Harper, 1937), p. 193.

[13] Quote from Ken Brown, "Washington Gladden: Exponent of Social Christianity" (unpublished Ph.D. dissertation, Duke University, 1964), p. 132.

[14] Rauschenbusch, p. 279.

[15] Brown, p. 120.

[16] Rauschenbusch, p. 222.

[17] *Ibid.,* p. 227.

[18] Reinhold Niebuhr, "Is Peace or Justice the Goal?" *The World Tomorrow,* XV, No. 10 (Sept. 21, 1932), 275-277.

[19] *Ibid.,* p. 275.

[20] *Ibid.,* p. 276.

[21] Reinhold Niebuhr, *Moral Man and Immoral Society* (New York: Scribner's, 1932), p. 223.

[22] Reinhold Niebuhr, "Pacifism and the Use of Force," *The World Tomorrow,* XI, No. 5 (May, 1928), 218-220.

[23] Obviously, he later gave up his international pacifism with the rise of the Nazi threat.

[24] *Ibid.,* p. 219.

[25] *Ibid.*

[26] *Ibid.,* p. 220.

[27] *Ibid.*

[28] Reinhold Niebuhr, "Marxism and Religion," *The World Tomorrow,* XVI, No. 11 (March, 1933), 253-255.

[29] *Ibid.,* p. 254.

[30] *Ibid.,* p. 255.

[31] *Ibid.,* p. 253.

32 *Ibid.,* p. 254.

33 Rauschenbusch, p. 184.

34 Max L. Stackhouse, "Toward a Theology for the New Social Gospel," *New Theology No. 4,* ed. by Martin E. Marty and Dean G. Peerman (Toronto: Macmillan, 1967), p. 221.

35 Frederick Herzog, "Political Theology," *The Christian Century,* LXXVI (July 23, 1969), 977.

36 Robert T. Handy, *The Social Gospel in America* (New York: Oxford, 1966), p. 11.

37 Staughton Lynd, "The Movement: A New Beginning," *Liberation* (May, 1969), p. 16.

Chapter VI

1 This statement was made not by a radical leftist but by an evangelical, Leighton Ford, in an address delivered on September 9, 1969, to the United States Congress on Evangelism at Minneapolis. The quotation may be found in "Evangelism in a Day of Revolution," *Christianity Today,* XIV (Oct. 24, 1969), 64.

2 S. G. F. Brandon, *Jesus and the Zealots* (Scribner's, 1967).

3 Walter Wink, "Jesus and Revolution," *Union Seminary Quarterly Review,* XXV (Fall, 1969), 55.

4 Johannes B. Metz, *Faith and the World of Politics* (New York: Paulist Press, 1968), p. 8.

5 This paper was read to the Chicago Society for Biblical Research in April, 1967, and is currently being expanded for publication. I am indebted to Yoder for the biblical references pointing to the messianic motif.

6 D. S. Russell, *Method and Message of Jewish Apocalyptic* (Philadelphia: Westminster, 1964), p. 16.

7 Graydon F. Snyder, "The Literalization of the Apocalyptic Form in the New Testament Church," *Biblical Research,* XIV (1969), 5.

8 Stanley Brice Frost, "Apocalyptic and History," *The Bible in Modern Scholarship,* ed. by J. Philip Hyatt (Nashville: Abingdon, 1965), p. 112.

9 Th. C. Vriezen, "Prophecy and Eschatology," *Supplements to Vetus Testamentum,* I (1953), 215.

10 Snyder, p. 6.

11 *Ibid.* For the problems at Corinth see pp. 8-15. For the problem at Thessalonica see pp. 15-18. The quotation is found on p. 7.

12 Richard Rubenstein, *After Auschwitz* (New York: Bobbs-Merrill, 1966).

13 Jan M. Lochman, "An Atheist Interpretation of the Bible," *Encounter,* XXX (Fall, 1969), 312.

NOTES

Chapter VII

[1] Richard Shaull, "Liberal and Radical in an Age of Discontinuity," *Christianity and Crisis,* XXIX (Jan. 5, 1970), 342.

[2] Moltmann, *Religion, Revolution, and the Future,* p. 141.

[3] J. Christian Beker, "Biblical Theology Today," *New Theology No. 6,* p. 31.

[4] Jan Lochman, "Ecumenical Theology of Revolution," *ibid.,* pp. 111-112.

[5] John Pairman Brown, *The Liberated Zone,* p. 87.

[6] Quoted in J. M. Lochman, "Ecumenical Theology of Revolution," *New Theology No. 6,* p. 114.

[7] James W. Douglass, *The Non-Violent Cross,* p. 9.

[8] John Pairman Brown, p. 103.

[9] Jacques Ellul, *Violence* (New York: Seabury, 1969), pp. 1237-141.

[10] *Ibid.,* pp. 160-67.

[11] Lochman, "Ecumenical Theology of Revolution," p. 115.

[12] Ellul, pp. 168-175.

[13] Letter from William Sloane Coffin, Jr., quoted by John A. T. Robinson, "Not Radical Enough?" *The Christian Century,* LXXXVI (November 12, 1969), 1449.

[14] Jürgen Moltmann, "Toward a Political Hermeneutics of the Gospel," *New Theology No. 6,* pp. 78-79.

[15] Arthur Gish, *The New Left and Christian Radicalism* (Grand Rapids: Eerdmans, 1970), p. 33.

[16] Quoted by Lochman, "Ecumenical Theology of Revolution," p. 107.

[17] Richard Shaull, "Christian Faith as Scandal in a Technocratic World," *New Theology No. 6,* p. 132.

[18] Rosemary Ruether, "The Free Church Movement Within Catholicism," *ibid.,* pp. 285-286.

[19] *Ibid.,* p. 286.

[20] See Emil Brunner, *The Christian Doctrine of the Church, Faith, and the Consummation* (Philadelphia: Westminster, 1962), pp. 4-133.

[21] Gish, p. 94.